The Necklace

DANIELA MASCETTI AND AMANDA TRIOSSI

The Necklace

From Antiquity to the Present

FOREWORD BY HUGH TAIT

HARRY N. ABRAMS, INC., PUBLISHERS

TO ALL OUR JEWELRY STUDENTS, TO BEATRICE AND TIMOTHY

FRONTISPIECE An Art Nouveau necklace by Georges Fouquet, *c.* 1904-5.
Photo courtesy of Sotheby's, Geneva (*see p. 126*).

Library of Congress Cataloging-in-Publication Data

Mascetti, Daniela.
    The necklace : from antiquity to the present / Daniela Mascetti
  and Amanda Triossi.
      p.   cm.
    Includes bibliographical references and index.
    ISBN 0-8109-3682-8 (clothbound)
    1. Necklaces—History.   I. Triossi, Amanda.   II. Title.
GT2260.M37   1997
391.7—DC21   96-48107

CONTENTS

FOREWORD

To trace the birth of the necklace is to start at the very beginning of the history of jewelry itself. At some unrecorded moment - for ever lost in the uncertainties of a pre-historic age - the profoundly human need for self-adornment led to ornamental objects being pierced, threaded and hung about the neck. Perhaps in the Garden of Eden, the first necklace was a daisy-chain - a precursor of those made by many a schoolgirl on a summer's day - but the demand for ornaments more lasting and more exotic than the flowers of the local meadow was not only fuelled by the extensive trading networks that, even in prehistoric times, had begun to cover vast areas of western Asia and Europe, but was itself a significant contributing factor in the expansion of these lines of trade. Indeed, beads of various materials are among the most common 'finds' from the excavations of prehistoric sites in the Middle East, and with the discovery in that part of the world of how to make both glazed faience and coloured glass beads, a new and plentiful supply of relatively inexpensive substitutes (loosely imitating the scarce coloured stones) became available for general trading purposes, and profit, across a gradually widening market. In the succeeding millennia, this pattern of development can be seen to be repeated, again and again, as new materials and new inventions become involved.

As a form, the necklace was so susceptible to change that, perhaps more than any other category of jewelry, it has benefited from man's discovery of new metals, new gemstones, new materials - even plastic - but, above all, from man's ingenious invention of new techniques that have enabled revolutionary new surface effects - as enamelling - to be created. The driving force has, undoubtedly, been a relentless desire for the excite-ment of originality and, if the primary goal was once to enhance the natural beauty of the wearer, then that objective has been abandoned or, at least, relegated to a very minor consideration in many instances.

Looking at the many necklaces that have survived from antiquity, it is tempting not only to speculate if any would have been specifically designed for the original recipient but also when, for the first time, the wearer's physical attributes were studied by the designer of a necklace before passing detailed instructions to the jeweler who was going to carry out the commission. If Greek mythology is to be believed, then the necklace which Harmonia, a daughter of Aphrodite, wore at her nuptials was a specially fash-ioned gift from Hephaestus, the Greek god of fire, but both Harmonia and her hus-band Cadmus, son of the king of Phoenicia, were so tormented by the misfortunes of their children that they entreated the gods to relieve them of the miseries of life and they were thereupon turned into serpents. Harmonia's necklace thus became famous for its reputation of being fatal to all who possessed it and, as with so many episodes in Greek mythology, the story reflects a social attitude towards the aspects of everyday life, particularly the age-old custom of placing amuletic necklaces on children to protect them from the various evils that caused so much fear among the peoples of the Ancient World.

The great advantage of the necklace has always been its flexibility. It could be enlarged as the wearer grew older; it could have more amuletic pendants or richer gemstones added to it as the wearer grew more prosperous. It could be easily repaired if part was lost or damaged, because a few new links or beads could replace those lost. For the collector and historian, these adaptations can create difficulties, but every necklace should be examined with human activity in mind. Because the repairer has only to copy in order to increase the number of elements within a necklace, it is often possible for his additions to be deceptively similar to the original. Many a necklace has had its original high-quality gemstones removed by a later owner and replaced by lesser stones of similar size but of less fire and colour. Even when a necklace itself has survived in an unaltered state, the large, separately-made, pendent jewels (found, for example, on Renaissance necklaces) are often later replacements for the lost originals and, through lack of sufficient expertise, these pastiches can strike a jarring note that detracts from the necklace as a whole.

The vast survey undertaken here by these two authors is a worthy sequel to their similar endeavour seven years ago when their subject was *Earrings from Antiquity to the Present*. Drawing upon the evidence in portraits, archival sources, workshop drawings and engraved designs, the authors have provided a framework within which they can discuss the qualities of each necklace they have chosen to include - and what a wonderfully rewarding assemblage of illustrations greets the reader of this book.

HUGH TAIT

AUTHORS' PREFACE

The principal aim of this survey is to give a chronological account of necklaces as they have been worn, mainly by women, from 30,000 B.C. until the present day, with the main emphasis being placed on the neck ornaments of the 19th and 20th centuries. Our concern has been to examine the shapes, principal designs and materials characteristic of each period and to relate them to the development of costume, with which they are inextricably linked.

The great extent and variety of the subject has meant that we have had to concentrate very much on examples from the mainstream of necklace design. However, the whole history of the necklace has been treated as far as possible, all types being analyzed in detail in the context of the periods in which they flourished. For instance, we look at pearl necklaces in detail in the chapter on the 17th century, since it was during this period that the single strand of pearls became by far the most fashionable form of neck ornament. Pearl necklaces, however, had been a constant feature of female adornment from the 3rd century B.C.; natural or, since the early 20th century, cultured pearls have been strung in a variety of ways throughout the ages and have been worn in single or multiple rows, close around the neck or hanging down. The basic design of such necklaces consists invariably of drilled gems strung on a thread, and we therefore felt that it was appropriate to give them rather less prominence in the chapters devoted to the necklace in more recent times, since the book does aim to focus on the evolution of design in neck ornament.

Throughout the history of the necklace, it is apparent that many styles have been created and recreated very much in the image of prevailing taste and contemporary fashion. We have therefore included a visual glossary of necklace and clasp types to demonstrate the elements of continuity from ancient times to the present day.

Much of the photographic material, especially of nineteenth- and twentieth-century pieces, has never been published before.

AMANDA TRIOSSI · DANIELA MASCETTI

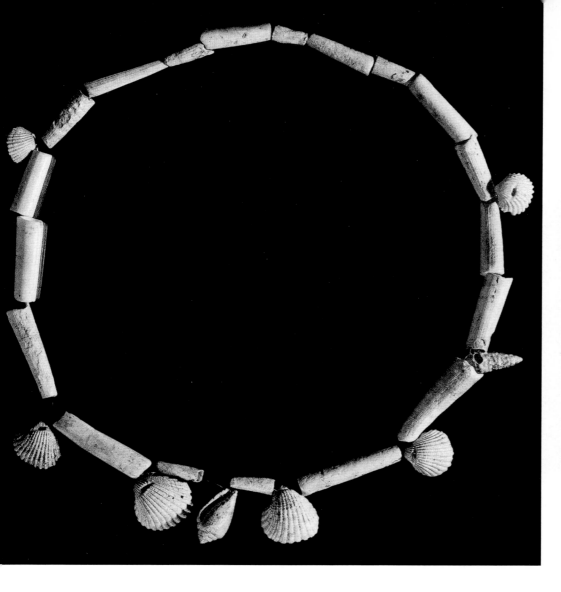

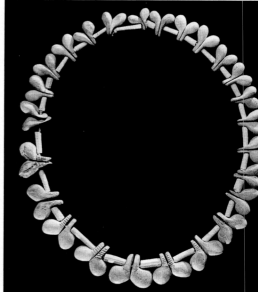

THE FIRST NECKLACES

This Palaeolithic necklace (*above*) made of various fossilized shell beads found at Pavlov, Czechoslovakia, dates from *c.* 28,000 B.C. Neolithic necklaces have been found in various forms: this example (*above right*) is of dentalium (a mollusc with a thinly pointed shell) and breast-shaped beads of bone, from El-Wad in the Jordan river valley, *c.* 10,000–8,000 B.C.; another example (*right*) of variously shaped cornelian beads and dentalium shells, *c.* 5800–5250 B.C., comes from Cyprus, as does the Bronze Age four-row necklace of white paste and red stone beads (*below*), which dates from *c.* 1900–1800 B.C.

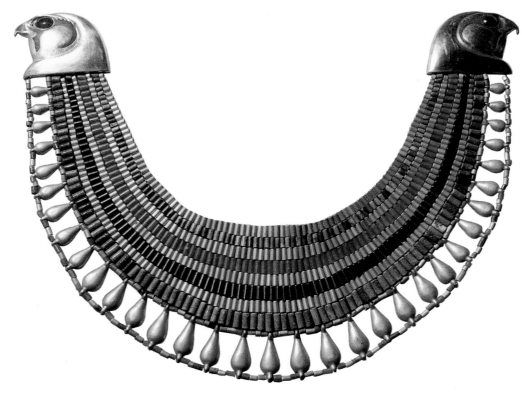

EGYPTIAN BROAD COLLARS
AND PECTORALS

Necklaces of vivid polychromy were highty appreciated in Ancient Egypt and worn by both men and women. The broad collar, which first appears during the 4th Dynasty (2613–2494 B.C.), was perhaps the most typical of all Egyptian jewels. The other notable form of neck ornament in Ancient Egypt was the pectoral, which had evolved from the primitive string and suspended pendant, to become the popular form of the 12th Dynasty (1991–1783 B.C.).

This pectoral from the treasure of Tutankhamun (*opposite left above*), designed as a golden bark carrying the electrum crescent and disc of the moon over the waters of the firmament, is decorated with polychrome glass inlays. The strap consists of four strings of gold and hardstone beads. Note the elaborate counterpoise. A somewhat earlier broad collar of turquoise, cornelian, green faïence and gold beads (*opposite below*) comes from the tomb of Seneb-tisi, 12th Dynasty; the falcon head terminals are made of thin gold foil filled with plaster. A painting (*left*) from the tomb of queen Nefertari, the wife of Ramesses II (1304–1237 B.C.) depicts the queen and the goddess Isis wearing broad collars of coloured beads and gold respectively. A much older panel (*right*) depicts Mentuhotep I (2060–2010 B.C.) wearing a polychrome bead broad collar, while similar ornaments are shown as being worn by the king and his queen Ankhesenamun on a casket lid (*below*) from the Tutankhamun treasure.

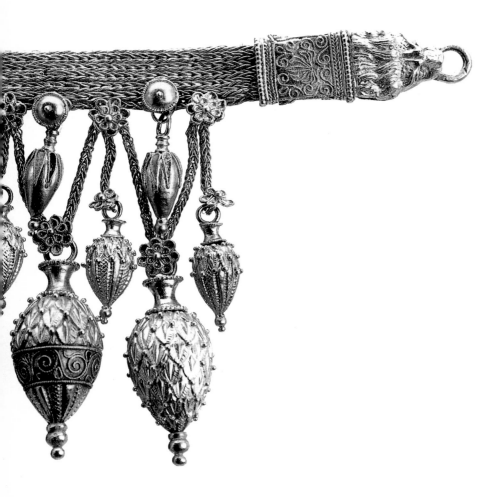

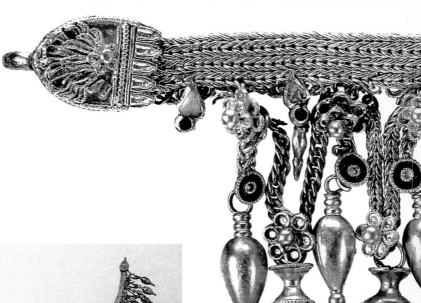

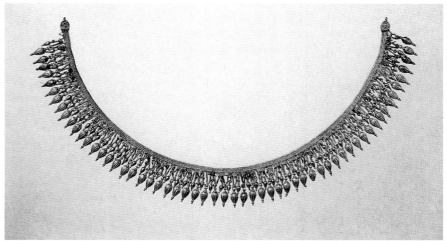

CLASSICAL GREEK

The most characteristic necklace of the Greek Classical period consisted of a row of flat elements, often rosettes alternating with palmettes, supporting three-dimensional pendants in the shape of seeds, acorns, buds and heads finely decorated with polychrome enamels and beaded wire details. The example from Pantikapeum (*opposite above, with detail*) dates from *c.* 400–380 B.C. and is typical of the style in vogue in the 5th and 4th centuries throughout the Greek world. It is designed as a chain of enamelled lotus-rosettes supporting drops in the shape of stylized seeds and achelous masks.

Around 340 B.C. a new type of necklace, the *plokion*, made its appearance; this consisted of a woven strap supporting a fringe of pendants of various designs, such as jar-shaped seeds, flower buds, and spear heads. In the most elaborate examples, the pendants are hung from intricate festoons of gold chains in different tiers. Joins in the chain-work are concealed by tiny gold elements such as discs and rosettes. The terminals of the straps usually take the form of mitre- or leaf-shaped elements. Fine filigree-work and polychrome enamels embellished the pendants which can be of different sizes and shapes.

This example (*above*), said to be from Melos, and that from Great Bliznitza (*left, with detail*), both dating from 330–300 B.C., are exceptional for their large scale, fine workmanship and detailing, but are otherwise typical of the period. These and similar examples served as a source of inspiration for many archaeological revival necklaces of the 19th century.

ETRUSCAN GOLD

The two fine necklaces illustrated on these pages are
typical of those popular in Etruria during the last decades
of the 6th century B.C. and at the beginning of the 5th,
which became the source of inspiration for many neck
ornaments produced in the late 19th century in the
archaeological revival style (*pp. 122–123*). This gold
necklace from Ruvo, southern Italy (*right*), *c.* 480 B.C.,
consists of a gold strap supporting pendants in the shape
of lotus flowers, acorns and satyr heads, richly decorated
with granulation. The satyr heads and the acorn drops
had a prophylactic function. The gold necklace from
Tuscany (*below, with detail*), *c.* 480–460 B.C., has a strap
supporting pendants in the shape of prophylactic
achelous heads, acorns, harpies, lotus flowers and is
set with onyx and amber in gold collets.

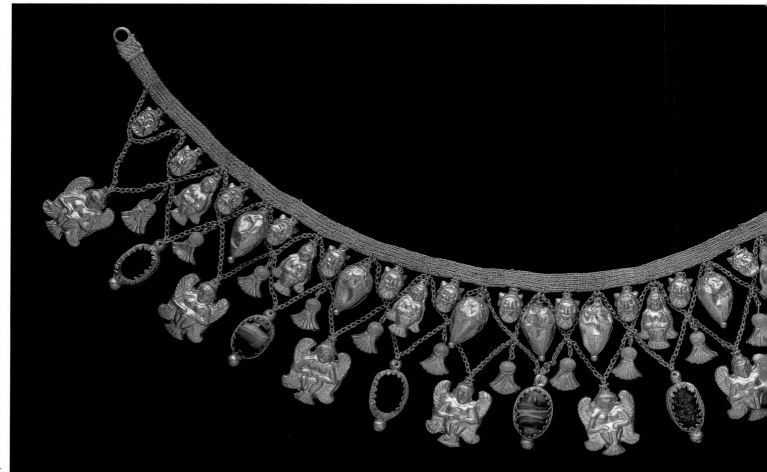

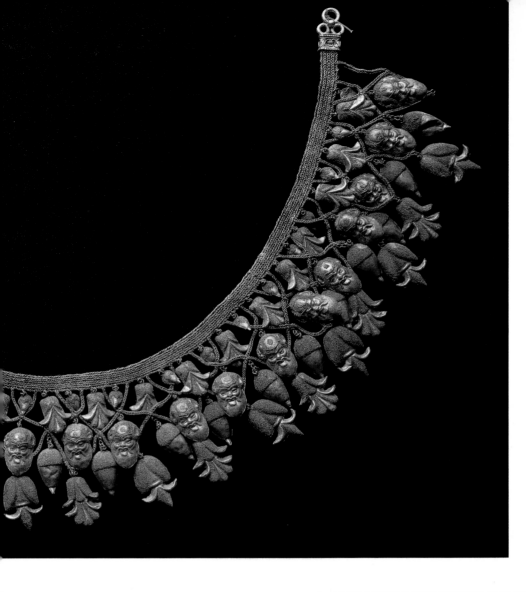

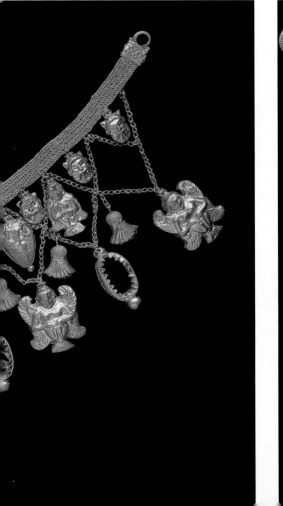

MINOAN AND MYCENAEAN

Necklaces were fashionable in the Minoan world in the form of strings of stone or gold beads. Their popularity during the Middle Minoan Period is confirmed by wall paintings from the island of Thera (modern Santorini), where women are depicted wearing several strings of differently shaped beads (*above*). In the 15th century B.C., the late Minoan and Early Mycenaean cultures produced a substantial number of necklaces formed of gold beads stamped out of sheet gold in shallow relief. Necklaces of this type remained fashionable throughout the Mycenaean world until the 12th century B.C. This necklace (*left*) of gold spiral-shaped elements comes from a tomb in Mycenae, *c.* 1400 B.C. A necklace from Cyprus (*below*) is formed of gold elements in the shape of figure-of-eight shields, 1400–1230 B.C.

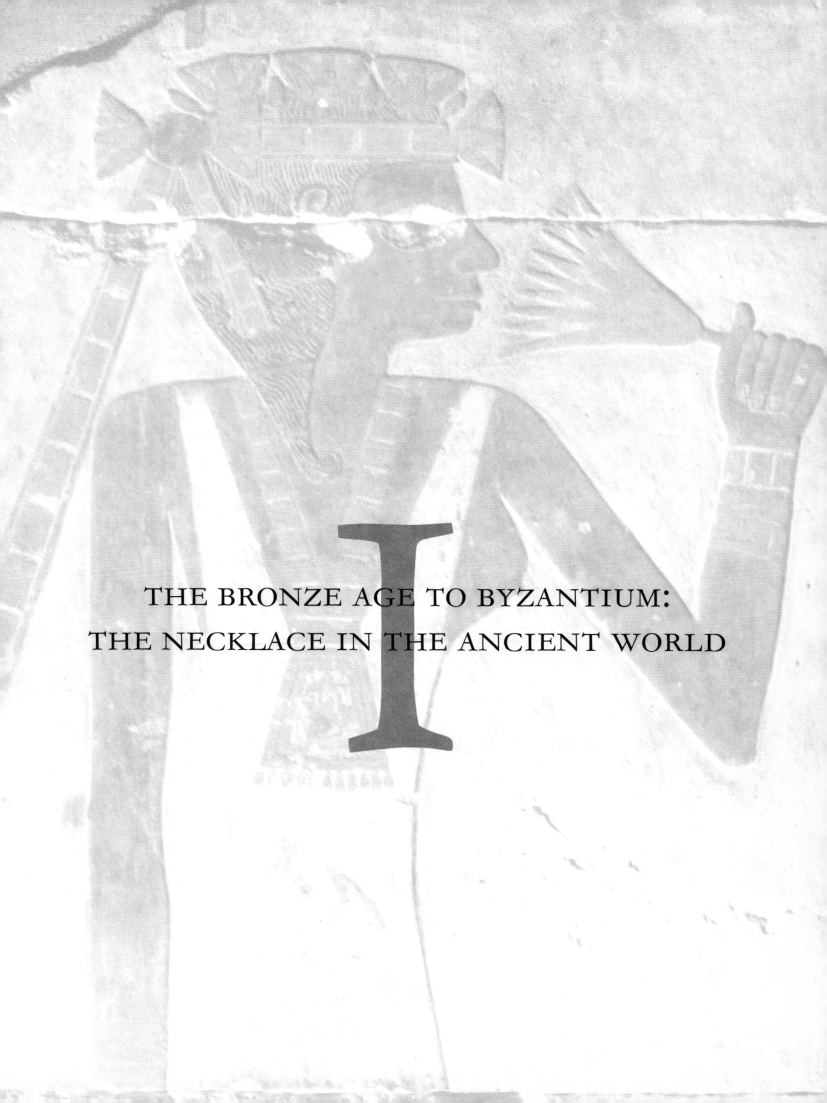

I

THE BRONZE AGE TO BYZANTIUM:
THE NECKLACE IN THE ANCIENT WORLD

*T*here is no more suitable place in the architecture of the human body to be adorned by a jewel than the base of the neck. From this position, the features of the face can be enhanced, the delicate curves of the shoulders underlined and the bust given striking adornment. Since the dawn of humanity men and women have understood the central decorative role of the necklace. In its simplest form – a string of perishable material from which are suspended rudimentary carved pendants of either ivory or bone – the necklace must be one of the earliest personal ornaments. Late Palaeolithic remains from as early as 30,000 B.C. indicate its use, although it is more than likely that at that period it was regarded as being more talismanic, prophylactic and amuletic than decorative (*see p. 9*). Necklaces made of strings of perforated shells, carved bones, fish vertebrae, animal teeth, claws and stone beads roughly polished and drilled, often arranged in several rows strung together and separated by larger spacer beads, have been found. It is interesting to consider that this simple primitive structure of a thread strung with a number of beads or pendants has remained the basis of the design for most necklaces through the ages until the present.

Ancient Sumer and Egypt

Necklaces consisting of perishable strings with beads of unbaked clay or mother-of-pearl, obsidian or polished and drilled stone, were among the most common ornaments for Sumerian men and women. Around 2500 B.C. necklaces for both sexes started to include gold elements. From a group of royal graves discovered in Ur – in present-day Iraq – have come several necklaces designed as strings of stone beads, lapis lazuli and cornelian, alternating with gold wire elements and leaf-shaped gold pendants. Chokers – short necklaces tightly encircling the column of the neck at its base – have also been found at the same site. One of the most extraordinary examples is made of triangular gold beads, alternating with similarly shaped lapis lazuli beads. Towards the end of the 3rd millennium B.C., Sumerian bead necklaces became more sophisticated, a process demonstrated by careful stringing to alternate and balance the different colours of stones and metal. Stone beads, capped and inlaid with gold, were also introduced.

A similar pattern of development from simple strings of beads to more elaborate compositions also characterized the evolution of the Egyptian necklace, culminating in the elaborate forms of the broad collar and of the pectoral. Early neck ornaments of Pre-dynastic and Early Dynastic periods (4th and 3rd millennia B.C.) consisted of simple strands of beads carved in stones such as cornelian, alternating with beads of glazed steatite. These were threaded on strings of perishable materials and, if not long enough to pass over the head, they were fastened at the back of the neck.

When and where gold was first discovered is not certain. Although it seems likely that the metal had been used in the composition of necklaces at an earlier date, the first archaeological findings of gold examples date to the 3rd millennium B.C. These were made in Sumerian and Egyptian areas, though gradually the craft spread from Western Asia to the Aegean and the Mediterranean.

It was not until the 4th Dynasty (2613–2494 B.C.) that gold beads started to be introduced into the design of simple string necklaces. At the same time, the more elaborate broad collar (*wesekh*) made its appearance (*see pp. 10-11*). This is perhaps the most typical of all Egyptian jewels; it was made up of several rows of cylindrical beads of stone or glazed composition, graduated in size and vertically strung in an open-circle design between terminals of semi-circular shape. Its lowermost row was most typically decorated either with leaf-shaped drops or mummiform beads. The earliest documentation of this ornament is on statues, but the first extant examples date from the 6th Dynasty (2323–2150 B.C.). Equally popular for men and women, the broad collar was worn in life and taken to the grave, or specifically made for funerary purposes. These collars, strung with multi-coloured stone beads alternating with gold elements, were so heavy that they required a counterpoise which, connected by means of strings of beads to the semi-circular terminal elements, rested on the back of the wearer, between the shoulder blades and kept the front element in place on the chest. The counterpoise is a typical feature of broad collars, and those found without must have been made for funerary purposes only. In more elaborate examples, the lunate or semi-circular terminals were substituted with lotus-flower motifs or falcon heads. Bright polychromy is a feature of Egyptian jewelry in general; vivid combinations of differently coloured beads, such as blue lapis lazuli, azure turquoise, red cornelian, purple amethyst, alternating with gold beads, characterize the design of many broad collars. They were also sometimes worn in conjunction with simple strings of beads which would be tied above it; confirmation of this is provided by wall frescoes and sarcophagi paintings.

During the 18th Dynasty (1550–1307 B.C.), real flowers, which it was customary to present to guests and which were thus frequently depicted in contemporary banqueting scenes, were simulated with collars of floral or foliate elements of brightly coloured glazed composition. The design of such pieces included elements in the forms of green leaves, red and blue bunches of grapes, white and yellow daisies, yellow mandrake fruits, white and mauve lotus flowers.

The other notable form of neck ornament in Ancient Egypt was the pectoral, which had evolved from the primitive string from which was suspended a pendant. The earliest representation of pectorals date back to the Old Kingdom (3rd millennium B.C.), but it is not until the 12th Dynasty (1991–1783 B.C.) that the pectoral designed as a trapezoidal pendant suspended from a string of beads became popular. The earliest extant examples consist of open-work pendants in the form of heraldic falcons decorated with a *cloisonné* inlay of semiprecious stones. This pendant later evolved into a royal jewel, taking the form of an open-work kiosk-shaped plaque, which enclosed the king's cartouche and included heraldic devices in the form of plants or animals. By the time of Tutankhamun (1333-1323 B.C.) the string of beads supporting the pectoral had evolved into a more elaborate bead strap, complete with counterpoise (*see pp. 10-11*).

Decorative techniques were also changing, the stone inlay being gradually substituted by glass. As in the case of the broad collar, pectorals were worn in life, taken to the grave, and often made especially for funerary purposes. These latter include designs of amuletic scarabs – or heart scarabs – inscribed with a magical formula text which bound the heart of the deceased to silence when it was weighed to ascertain if its master was worthy of entering the Egyptian paradise.

It is not surprising that the decorative value of these magnificent and brightly coloured neck ornaments was especially appreciated in Ancient Egypt, especially when considered in relation to contemporary costume. This consisted mainly of fitted white linen garments, which finished below the breast and were kept in place by shoulder straps, for women, and loin cloths for men. The colours, bold shapes and precious materials of neck ornaments provided a needed decorative element for styles which left the upper part of the body completely exposed in the case of both sexes. It is hardly surprising, then, that when a system of awards was instituted in the New Kingdom, the most prestigious element of the award was a necklace (the *shebyu* collar) designed as four rows of gold, disc-shaped beads, which the king placed around the neck of those subjects he wished to honour.

It is interesting to note that the necklaces produced in Egypt during the Ptolemaic Period conformed to Hellenistic designs, losing their characteristic Egyptian polychromy and form. The traditional shapes and colours survived only on painted coffins.

The Minoan and Mycenaean Civilizations

The craft of working in gold spread gradually from Western Asia towards the Mediterranean, reaching the Aegean in about 2400 B.C. The earliest evidence of the employment of gold in the manufacture of necklaces there is provided by the discovery of beads of various shapes dating from *c.* 2200 B.C., which have been found on the Greek mainland and on Crete, centre of Early Minoan culture. Early Minoan ladies adorned their necks with bead necklaces of cornelian, amethyst, faïence, steatite and shell, enhanced with gold elements of globular, cylindrical, disc, drum or biconical shape. During the Middle Minoan Period, between 2000 and 1600 B.C., more elaborate bead shapes were introduced, such as lotus flowers and lilies, and cords or simple gold chains were threaded with realistically modelled animal forms such as lions, fish, birds and insects (*see p. 16*). These are well represented in wall paintings from the isle of Thera – the modern Santorini – then under the influence of Crete. Women are here often depicted wearing several bead necklaces graduated in length, at times made up of simple beads, at times of more elaborate zoomorphic forms.

In the 15th century B.C., however, the Late Minoan and Early Mycenaean cultures started to produce brilliant necklaces of new and varied design. Particularly abundant on the mainland, these necklaces were designed as rows of gold beads or other elements stamped out of sheet gold in shallow relief, backed with a flat sheet of gold, with the space between filled with material to add weight. According to their shape and size, the beads were pierced in one or more places for stringing. The best examples are frequently decorated with granulation and occasionally highlighted with touches of blue enamel. The subject-matter of these necklace elements, often of naturalistic inspiration, is extremely varied. Volutes, curved leaves, ivy leaves, palm leaves, rosettes, flowerheads, shells, pomegranates, argonauts, papyrus, figure-of-eight shields are among the shapes found next to the lotus and lily of the Middle Minoan examples.

The abundance of archaeological remains seems to suggest a form of mass-production; although increasingly reproduced in glass, such necklace elements remained popular throughout the Mycenaean world until the 12th century B.C. Similar necklaces, designed as rows of figure-of-eight shields and pomegranates, have been excavated in Cyprus, where they seem to have been popular during the Cypro-Mycenaean period (1400–1050 B.C.).

By about 1100 B.C. the Mycenaean civilization had begun to collapse, apparently under the pressure of a series of invasions. Three centuries of poverty and near-barbarism followed: all forms of art declined in this period, known as the Dark Ages, and jewelry was no exception. Ornaments made of precious metals became rare, and it is likely that most of the few that were produced were manufactured with gold looted from Mycenaean tombs. The little gold jewelry which has survived from this period is of the simplest kind, made of gold wire. It includes finger rings, spiral bracelets, smaller spiral jewels, some earrings and hair ornaments. Gold necklaces seem to be totally absent.

Ancient Greece

Towards the end of the 9th century B.C., contacts between Western Asia and Greece were resumed and approximately two centuries of Oriental influence on Greek art followed. Cyprus and Syria – taken in the broadest sense to include Phoenicia and the Neo-Hittite North Syria – were the two principal influences on Greece, Syria acting as a channel for Egyptian and Mesopotamian influences. It is likely that craftsmen from these countries – famous for their goldsmiths – settled in Greece and taught their arts to local apprentices. Many jewels of this period show a clear resemblance to Mycenaean artefacts, and since there was a continuity of tradition on the Greek mainland, it has to be assumed that Mycenaean fashions and techniques, kept alive in Syria and Cyprus during the Dark Ages, were reintroduced to the Greek world about this time.

Gold jewels are relatively abundant in this period and generally of high quality. This fact is certainly related to the opening up of the East to the Greek world through colonization, giving access to rich sources of precious metal in Asia Minor, especially to the Lydian gold mines. Old goldsmith techniques, such as granulation and filigree, were revived or perfected in this period. New techniques, such as inlaying with stone, amber and glass, were also introduced. Under Oriental influence, casting and *repoussé*-work

A Greek gold necklace designed as a succession of rosettes supporting a fringe of acorn-shaped motifs, 5th century B.C.

were mastered, the latter applied increasingly to stout sheets of gold. Necklaces made of gold beads of globular, lenticular, bud, melon, and biconical shapes are well represented both on the mainland and on the Greek islands. The most characteristic form of neck ornament of the time, though, is a collar formed of several gold plaques, rectangular or trapezoid in shape, decorated with embossed figures, and generally fitted with gold tubular elements along the upper edge to take a suspension cord. This was most probably secured to the dress at shoulder height by means of hooks.

The most striking of these plaques came from the island of Rhodes and date from the second half of the 7th century B.C. Their subject-matter is mainly of Phoenician and Mycenaean inspiration, and includes the Phoenician goddess Astarte, winged representations of Artemis as mistress of beasts, with animals at her sides, and sphinxes. Neck ornaments constructed along the lines of similarly embossed gold plaques and dating from 700–600 B.C. have also been excavated in Cyprus, and the presence on the island of similar but simpler, less refined plaques dating from the 8th and 9th centuries B.C. seems to suggest a Cypriot origin for this form of ornament.

Greek jewelry of the 6th and early 5th centuries B.C. – the Archaic Period – is generally of high quality and considerable artistic brilliance, but very little has survived (*see p. 33*). It is, however, amply documented in contemporary sculpture and vase painting; it seems that the scarcity of gold at the time caused it to be replaced in the manufacture of jewels by silver and bronze, metals that cannot be expected to survive as well. Necklaces from the 6th century B.C. are very rare; the few beads and pendants which have survived suggest very little change from those of the 7th century.

It was not until the Persian wars that gold became more plentiful in Greece. It is interesting to note that Greek Classical jewelry is better known from examples from southern Russia, Cyprus and southern Italy than from Greece proper, where gold was probably relatively rare in the private sector and where sumptuary laws restricting the use of gold were well established. There was, however, a great variety of jewelry and, among the abundance of diadems, earrings, bracelets and finger rings, the presence of necklaces is well documented. Apart from archaeological findings, the popularity and the designs of necklaces are amply represented in contemporary sculpture, terracotta figurines, vase paintings and even on coinage. Literary sources mentioning jewels are rarer, but texts concerning the works of Pheidias, and especially his chryselephantine statues, confirm the popularity of necklaces, especially those designed as a succession of rosettes supporting fringes of pendants. The famous sculpture of the Athena Parthenos included several such examples. The elaborate designs of Greek necklaces of the 5th century B.C., the Classical period, included many of the beads popular in previous centuries, arranged in a more elaborate manner.

There are two main styles of necklace dating from the 5th century B.C. The first, a continuation of types popular in the 6th century, consisted of a row of gold sheet beads of uniform design – spherical, lenticular, tubular, variously decorated with ribbed patterns, filigree and granulation – often alternating with or supporting beads designed as fruits, seeds or buds and occasionally with a larger, animal head pendant at the centre (*see p. 33*). The second and perhaps the most characteristic type was designed as a row of flatter elements, often rosettes alternating with palmettes, supporting three-dimensional pendants in the shape of seeds, acorns, buds and female heads. In necklaces of this type the gold sheet-work is finely decorated with beaded wire details, but most striking is the vibrant effect obtained by the play of light and shade on differently reflecting surfaces of flat, concave and convex gold sheet. This particular type remained in vogue during the 4th century B.C. throughout the Greek world.

As many as seven words for necklaces were used in the Greek language: *hormos*, *hormiskos*, *kathema*, *hypoderis*, *halysion*, *plokion* and *katheter*. The first four seem to refer to necklaces made of repeated elements, while *halysion* is more likely to refer to an ornament made of different elements. The *plokion*, a term first used in temple inventories *c.* 340 B.C., made its appearance at the end of the Classical period (*see pp. 12-13*). It consisted of a woven strap supporting a fringe of pendants of various design. This type rapidly became fashionable and remained popular for some two centuries. It is certainly the most characteristic form of neck ornament of the Hellenistic period, from the Greek mainland to eastern Greece, and from southern Italy to southern Russia. Thanks to Alexander the Great's conquests in the Orient, gold poured into Greece as spoils of war and from exploitation of mines in the conquered territories. Jewels were thus produced in great abundance and many examples survive to this day.

The simplest examples of the strap necklace consist of ribbons which look at first sight to be plaited, but are actually made of very fine gold chains linked together side by side, supporting a fringe of small pendants (*see pp. 12-13*). In more elaborate examples, the pendants are hung from intricate festoons of gold chains in different tiers. Joins in the chain-work are concealed by tiny gold elements such as discs and rosettes, usually of very fine workmanship and decorated with filigree. Traces of the green, blue and white enamel that once lavishly decorated many of these necklaces is still preserved in some examples. The shapes of the pendants, which in the more elaborate pieces were of two or three different sizes, are of two main types. The first includes jar-shaped seeds and flower buds, while the second type consists of spear heads. The latter, which most recent research tends to interpret as beech-nut forms rather than spear heads, did not evolve in its design. On the other hand, the jar outlines of seed-like or flower bud-like pendants, gradually transformed themselves into amphora-shaped drops with well-defined necks. The terminals of the straps usually take the form of mitre- or leaf-shaped elements decorated with foliage, rosettes or palmettes in gold wire. Lion-head terminals, finely chased and detailed, are rare, but have been found along the southern coast of Crimea.

Another necklace which was popular throughout the Hellenistic period is the chain, loose linked or corded, terminating in animal heads. The most common decorative motif for the terminals is the lion head, but variants with dolphin, antelope and negro heads are also known. Often variously coloured glass beads or beads carved in stones such as garnets were set at intervals between the gold links. This type was particularly popular in southern Italy, from where magnificent examples survive.

A fringe necklace shown on a portable bronze container in the form of a female head, Etruscan, c. 200–150 B.C.

A female terracotta votive statue, Lavinium, 4th century B.C., showing the form of the *bulla* and the pectoral (*see p. 27*).

Yet another type of necklace came into popularity in eastern Greece at the end of the 4th century B.C. It consists of two long corded chains passing through a large biconical slide bead decorated with filigree, each terminating in a tassel of thinner chains decorated with variously shaped pendants.

In Classical and Hellenistic times necklaces were certainly made with the primary aim of enhancing the beauty of the wearer, but they were also intended to reveal status and wealth, as well as sentimental, religious and amuletic significance. They were in fact part of the precious paraphernalia with which the statues of gods were embellished, but they have also been recorded in the inventories of sanctuaries as thanksgiving offerings. Necklaces were worn by women in life and followed them to their graves. Although a number of marble sculptures of the early 6th century B.C. from Attica seem to suggest that men wore necklaces or some form of neck ornaments, by the middle of the century it was generally considered improper and effeminate for Greek men to wear any jewel other than finger rings or gold wreaths on special occasions.

Vase paintings and terracotta statues are of great help to our understanding of the popularity of necklaces in Classical and Hellenistic times and of how they were worn. Fashionable clothing which consisted mainly of a tunic, the *chiton*, formed of draped material clasped at the shoulders, required the wearing of necklaces tight around the neck or, more comfortably, loosely tied at its base. Often worn in multiples, a favourite combination of necklaces was that of a simple string of beads worn high on the neck, above a more elaborate necklace of beads and pendants. It is sometimes assumed that the shortest examples were worn across the breast, pinned or, more likely, directly sewn on the *chiton*. It is more probable, however, that these short examples were tied at the back with strings.

Throughout the Classical period necklaces were fastened by means of tying the cord on which the elements were strung. Even the strap necklaces of the Hellenistic period were fastened in this way, the cord being threaded through the rings fitted at each terminal. Around 300 B.C. some necklaces started to be fitted with a ring at one end and with a hook at the other (*see pp. 36-37*). This type of fastening obviously meant that necklaces had to be longer in order to encircle the neck and had to be made to measure. This more costly way of producing necklaces was undoubtedly a consequence of the greater availability of gold for personal ornament which followed the conquests of Alexander the Great. In particular, the ring-and-hook fastening becomes a feature of those Hellenistic necklaces designed as chains of gold links and beads with zoomorphic terminals which were particularly popular in southern Italy. In such examples, the zoomorphic and hook-and-eye fastening became a decorative device possibly worn at the front.

The Etruscans

The earliest remains of Etruscan civilization in central Italy date from the end of the 8th century B.C. The great wealth of the Etruscans, attributable largely to the mineral resources of the country, is reflected in the sumptuousness of their tombs. In female graves, vessels of precious metal and silver and gold jewelry, such as necklaces, fibulae, pectorals and earrings, reflect not only the important role of women in society but also jewelry's function as retained wealth. Although Etruscan art was remarkably free of Greek influences in its earliest manifestations, it did not long remain so, and by the end of the 7th century B.C. Greek influence was becoming increasingly significant. Etruscan art, however, never lost its identity completely.

The earliest form of neck ornament of the Etruscan world was a string of variously shaped gold, silver and electrum beads, often supporting amber, glass-paste or faïence pendants or medallion-shaped *bullae*. The *bulla*, a jewel worn by women and children, was popular during the late Iron Age and continued in great favour during the 7th

The form of an elaborate Etruscan pectoral and the *bulla* on a votive statue, Lavinium, 4th century B.C.

century B.C., the period of Oriental influence (*see pp. 34-35*). In its simplest and earliest form it consists of disc-shaped pendants made of gilt-bronze sheet or gold sheet with embossed decoration in concentric bands. The earliest examples were decorated exclusively with geometrical motifs: dots, concentric circles, S-shaped and V-shaped motifs or meanders. The quantity of finds all over Etruscan territory, dating from as early as the last decades of the 8th century B.C., confirms the popularity of this ornament. Its main function was probably amuletic and not necessarily related to rank, since similar examples have been found in graves whose contents reflect burials of different social standing.

Similar pendants from the second half of the 8th century B.C. have been found on Rhodes, and both types seem to share an Oriental origin. The *bulla* continued in great favour during the 7th century, when its decorative repertoire began to show a more complex and varied selection of motifs, such as palmettes, rosettes, zoomorphic and anthropomorphic figures, sun discs and moon crescents of clear Oriental inspiration. In terms of technique, granulation, which reached the highest standards under the Etruscans, either complemented or provided a substitute for embossed decoration. It seems that, for some reason, during the 6th century B.C. and the first half of the 5th century, *bulla* pendants became unfashionable. Towards the end of the 5th century, however, they came back into vogue, together with large gold pendants in the shape of apotropaic lions and gorgons, satyrs, young male and female heads, hollow inside to allow the storage of perfumed oils. But it was not until the mid 4th century that the circular *bulla* made a triumphal return in the shape of large lenticular or, less frequently, heart-shaped pendants of plain or embossed gold sheet.

The decorative repertoire included, together with the prophylactic heads of satyrs and gorgons and mythological scenes involving the Greek pantheon. It is interesting to note that while women wore *bullae* decorated with subjects relating to female goddesses, young boys bore those relating to the male pantheon. Although a strong Greek influence is noticeable in the decorative subject-matter, the jewelry itself is totally Etruscan and has practically no counterpart in Greece. Several examples of necklaces mounted with three, five or seven *bullae* are known, but the most widespread fashion required girls, women and young men to wear one alone on a cord or gold chain. *Bullae* continued in favour in Etruria during the following centuries and the fashion only declined in early Roman Imperial times.

Etruscan necklaces of the 7th century B.C., whether designed as chains of gold mesh, of simple circular links or made of variously shaped beads, plain or decorated with granulation, often supported pendants of extremely varied and exotic deign. Apart from the *bullae*, pendants designed as lilies, amphorae, melons, acorns, anchors and female busts of clear Oriental influence were widely used. These pendants, like the *bullae*, were generally fitted at the top with a tubular element for threading. Another popular pendant, which appeared around 700 B.C., consisted of scarabs swivelling within a gold or silver mount. Originally imported from Phoenician and North Syrian areas, such pendants were very quickly imitated by Etruscan workshops which substituted the Oriental seals with scarab-like carvings in rock crystal and amber. Multi-coloured glass beads of Phoenician origin were also often used as pendants.

Another class of neck ornament, although not strictly speaking a necklace, needs to be mentioned here: the pectoral. This can be considered one of the most typical Etruscan ornaments, and was probably a status symbol indicating wealth and rank among Etruscan notables of the late 8th and first half of the 7th century B.C. Generally semicircular or rectangular, pectorals were decorated with patterns of geometrical and Oriental inspiration, embossed from gold sheet and, like the *bulla*, they have been found in both female and male graves. This fact, together with tomb wall-paintings, terracotta figures and sarcophagi lids, confirms that, in Etruscan culture, largely indebted to the Orient for its taste for luxury and opulence, it was perfectly acceptable for men to wear jewels, and that neck ornaments were particularly favoured.

During the 6th and early 5th centuries B.C. the Etruscan jewelers concentrated on the introduction of hardstones and glass pastes into the decoration of jewelry. Filigree and granulation continued to be used and contributed to exciting pictorial and chromatic effects. Necklaces were either very simple in design or extremely elaborate. Among the simplest were those designed as chains of spherical gold beads decorated with filigree and granulation floral motifs, alternating with plain circular gold beads. More elaborate were those of gold-mesh chains supporting differently shaped beads. Acorn-shaped beads were especially popular; they were occasionally hollow and fitted with minute lids, perhaps because they were intended to contain perfumed oils. Apotropaic pendants in the shape of achelous or satyr heads were also common and remained popular throughout the 4th century. Sirens, lion heads, winged creatures and amphorae were popular, together with talismanic animal tusks or arrow heads capped with gold filigree mounts.

The most stunning and elaborate necklaces, however, were those created during the last decades of the 6th and at the beginning of the 5th centuries (*see pp. 14-15*). These examples were designed as gold straps supporting a network of looped chains from which were suspended variously shaped elements: rosettes, discs, palmettes, lotus flowers, acorns, sirens, gorgons, satyr heads, scarabs and, occasionally, hardstones, especially agates and cornelians, set in gold collets. Their straps were generally fitted with looped terminals for attachment to a cord to be tied at the back of the neck. Greek influence is very strong in these necklaces, but although design and ornamental details are of Hellenic origin, the final result remains typically Etruscan, only refined in its forms and contents by positive contact with the Greek artistic language. It is interesting to note that it is precisely this type of strap necklace, supporting a fringe of variously designed pendants, which became the main inspiration for many of necklaces produced during the late 19th century in the archaeological revival style.

For the last three decades of the 4th century B.C., Etruscan jewelry moved definitively into the sphere of Hellenistic influence. The most popular necklaces of this period are those common throughout the Hellenic world, designed as gold straps supporting a fringe of small pendants of different shapes. Locally made in imitation of Hellenistic prototypes or directly imported from Hellenized centres, this type is better known from terracotta sculptures than from extant examples. The votive terracotta statues from Lavinium are, in this respect, of great help: they portray life-size figures of young men and women celebrating their passage from childhood to adult age with an offering to a divinity. They wear ceremonial dresses and hold offerings, toys and small animals in their hands. They all wear jewels in abundance: the males wear bead necklaces supporting *bullae*, while female figures are lavishly adorned with earrings, *bullae*, pectorals and strap necklaces. This last type of neck ornament is also popular on terracotta lids of the 3rd and 2nd centuries B.C. depicting deceased noble Etruscan ladies wearing jewels, among which strap necklaces are almost invariably present.

Celtic Europe

The torc, or rigid neck ring, is probably the most typical form of body ornament of the Celtic cultures which stretched from the British Isles to France and Spain in the West and eastward to the Germanic lands during the last five centuries of the first millennium B.C. (*see pp. 42-43*). The origins of this ornament go back to the Middle Bronze Age, when bronze and gold examples designed as twisted bars of cruciform section with hooked terminals were seen purely in Britain, Ireland and Northern France. Whether these torcs were seen purely as jewelry or not is still unclear; there are strong possibilities that their main function was that of special-purpose currency, since their weight appears to have been a multiple of what has been recently recognized as a unit of weight used by the Celts. From the 4th century B.C. onwards, the most popular form of torc was designed as an open ring of tubular section, solid or hollow, made of sheet gold, and decorated at the two ends with variously shaped terminals. Examples made of two or more bars of circular section, twisted together with looped terminals, have also been found. It is interesting to note that, although the accounts of Classical authors mention torcs as being worn by warriors in battle, the archaeological findings in graves are mainly associated with female burials. Examples found in hoards, especially in Britain, besides having a decorative and symbolic function, may also have had a specific value for their metal content and acted as a form of currency.

The Roman and Byzantine Empires

Examples of silver and gold jewelry from pre-Republican and Republican Rome are very scarce. From those that survive we can conclude that between 700 and 250 B.C. Roman jewelry was, for all practical purposes, Etruscan. Material is even scarcer for the period between 250 and 27 B.C., but it is likely that Roman jewelry, like the Etruscan, followed Hellenistic models.

For many centuries, jewelry was a luxury looked upon with official disapproval in the Roman world. The amounts of gold which could be buried with the dead and which a Roman woman could wear were fixed by law. Moreover, certain items of personal adornment, such as finger rings, were strictly limited to certain social classes and for certain occasions. An exception to the sumptuary laws of the 3rd century B.C. was the gold *bulla*, the pendant of Etruscan origin. In 210 B.C., the consul Levinus encouraged the senators to give the state treasury all the bronze, silver and gold they possessed, keeping only the *bulla* for their eldest son and an ounce of gold for the adornment of the women of the house. Tradition says that the *bulla* was first introduced to Rome by Tarquinius Priscus, the Etruscan king, who gave it as a present to his fourteen-year-old son who had distinguished himself in the wars against the Sabines. The *bulla*, or *aurum Etruscum* as Juvenal first called it, was worn in Republican Rome by children, young men and women. Its popularity continued among the peoples of the Italian peninsula until the 2nd century A.D., with little change from the designs developed in Etruria.

By 27 B.C., when the Roman Empire was established, Rome had finally absorbed what remained of the Hellenistic world with the annexation of Egypt in 30 B.C. These political events, however, had little impact on the minor arts, and during the first years of the Empire jewelry continued to be produced in Hellenistic forms. The major centres of jewelry manufacture were the traditional ones of Alexandria and Antioch, followed by Rome itself, where a large number of craftsmen from the East had settled and taught their skills to local goldsmiths. Progressively, wealth, luxury and ostentation as ideals replaced Republican sobriety; jewelry and personal adornment now became an important feature in Roman life, though necklaces produced in this period differed little from those of Hellenistic design. Gold chains of different linking remained very popular, often set at intervals with stone beads; an innovation of the late 1st century A.D. was the inclusion in the design of a wheel motif, either as a pendant or as a finial.

From the 1st century onwards, Roman jewelry began to distance itself in techniques and materials from Hellenistic models and to forge a distinct identity. Jewelers increasingly made greater use of coloured gemstones which provided them with a much wider palette. Around the end of the 2nd century, a gold-piercing technique, commonly but erroneously described as *opus interassile*, was introduced. This completely transformed the look of gold jewelry, imparting a lace-like quality which contrasted starkly with the unbroken gold surfaces of earlier jewels.

After this development, necklaces began to be set with a larger number of gemstones, such as emeralds, aquamarines, garnets, sapphires, rock crystal and topazes. These were usually cut in circular or rectangular shapes and simply polished in *cabochon* form, and combined with pearls for striking chromatic effect. The most popular of all colour combinations was probably that of purple amethysts, green emeralds or plasma – a green variety of chalcedony – with pearls and gold. In design, the favoured style consisted of a chain of differently coloured gemstones, mounted in wide rimmed gold bezels and connected to each other by means of small gold links. A development of this type, which first appeared around the year A.D. 200, consisted of similar chains of coloured gemstones alternating with gold decorative links, pierced in gold sheet in different patterns (*see pp. 40-41*).

Gold chains of various linkings remained popular throughout the 3rd and 4th centuries, though these were now enriched with pendants in the form of either single gemstones, or glass pastes in wide-rimmed gold bezels, gold coins, or medallions in simple or elaborate gold frames. Gold link chains were often interspersed with gemstone beads or, more typically, with uncut emeralds in their crystalline form of hexagonal prisms, drilled lengthways and threaded on gold wire.

All evidence indicates that, during the 2nd and 3rd centuries A.D., necklaces were worn in great profusion throughout the Roman Empire. For example, the funerary reliefs from Palmyra in Syria show more than one necklace being worn simultaneously. Often, as many as four or five necklaces of different length and design were worn to cover the bust from the base of the neck to just above the waist.

Most necklaces of the period of Imperial Rome were fitted with variously designed hook-and-eye fastenings; some of the most important and expensive examples had a circular or domed clasp-like element mounted at one end, variously decorated in relief or set with gemstones, and provided with a gold loop through which was passed the hook mounted at the other end.

One of the consequences of the disintegration of the Roman Empire in the west and the survival of the eastern Empire, ruled from Constantinople, was that once more Oriental taste came to influence Western art. In jewelry, however, Roman techniques and forms continued to be dominant; the lace-like effects of many Byzantine jewels are only a logical development of Roman pierced-work (*see pp. 38-39*). A clear example of this can be found in the most common form of Byzantine necklace, which consisted of a chain of discs fretted in various patterns. This style became especially popular in the 6th and 7th centuries.

Another typical feature of Roman jewelry, the use of large coloured gemstones, both precious and semiprecious, continued to be a characteristic of Byzantine work. Necklaces designed as chains of variously shaped gold links interspersed with pearls and coloured gemstones were typical. These had large circular gold medallions suspended from them, either fretted in open-work patterns and set with gemstones, or decorated with polychrome *cloisonné* enamels. Chains decorated at the two ends with circular finial plaques fretted in gold sheet in various patterns were also popular. The two circular decorative elements were provided with a hook and an eye respectively for fastening. However, examples with only one end decorated with the circular element are also known. This continuation of Roman forms in the Byzantine period can partly be explained by the lack of evolution in dress, where the simple tunic continued to be the principal garment of attire.

THE NECKLACE IN THE GREEK WORLD

The designs of necklaces in the Greek world from the 6th century B.C. onwards are amply represented in contemporary sculpture, terracotta figurines, vase painting and even on coinage. This Attic red-figure hydria (*below, with detail*) attributed to the Methyse Painter, *c.* 450 B.C., depicts a woman holding a necklace.

The design of this neck ornament is close to that of the gold necklace (*above*), said to be from Akarnania, *c.* 450–400 B.C.; it is made of a row of spherical beads alternating with myrtle-bud pendants. It is a good example of the simpler of the two types of neck ornament in vogue in Greece during the Classical period, which consisted of a row of gold sheet beads of uniform design, alternating with or supporting beads designed as fruits, seeds or buds.

33

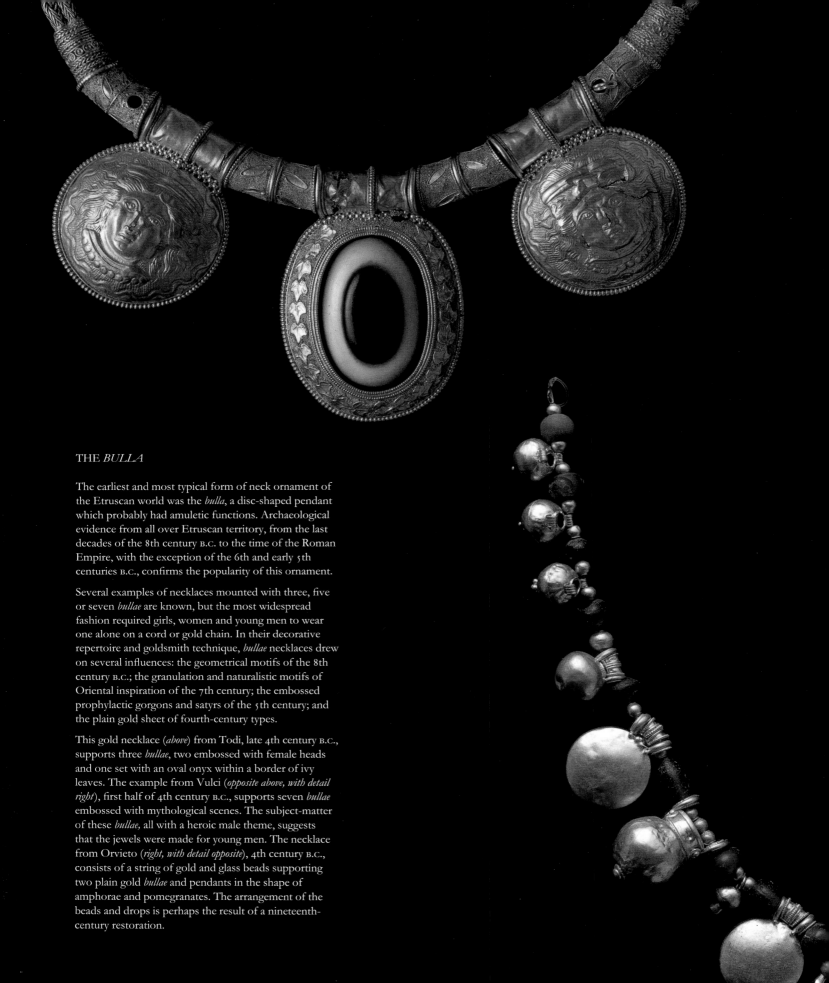

THE *BULLA*

The earliest and most typical form of neck ornament of the Etruscan world was the *bulla*, a disc-shaped pendant which probably had amuletic functions. Archaeological evidence from all over Etruscan territory, from the last decades of the 8th century B.C. to the time of the Roman Empire, with the exception of the 6th and early 5th centuries B.C., confirms the popularity of this ornament.

Several examples of necklaces mounted with three, five or seven *bullae* are known, but the most widespread fashion required girls, women and young men to wear one alone on a cord or gold chain. In their decorative repertoire and goldsmith technique, *bullae* necklaces drew on several influences: the geometrical motifs of the 8th century B.C.; the granulation and naturalistic motifs of Oriental inspiration of the 7th century; the embossed prophylactic gorgons and satyrs of the 5th century; and the plain gold sheet of fourth-century types.

This gold necklace (*above*) from Todi, late 4th century B.C., supports three *bullae*, two embossed with female heads and one set with an oval onyx within a border of ivy leaves. The example from Vulci (*opposite above, with detail right*), first half of 4th century B.C., supports seven *bullae* embossed with mythological scenes. The subject-matter of these *bullae*, all with a heroic male theme, suggests that the jewels were made for young men. The necklace from Orvieto (*right, with detail opposite*), 4th century B.C., consists of a string of gold and glass beads supporting two plain gold *bullae* and pendants in the shape of amphorae and pomegranates. The arrangement of the beads and drops is perhaps the result of a nineteenth-century restoration.

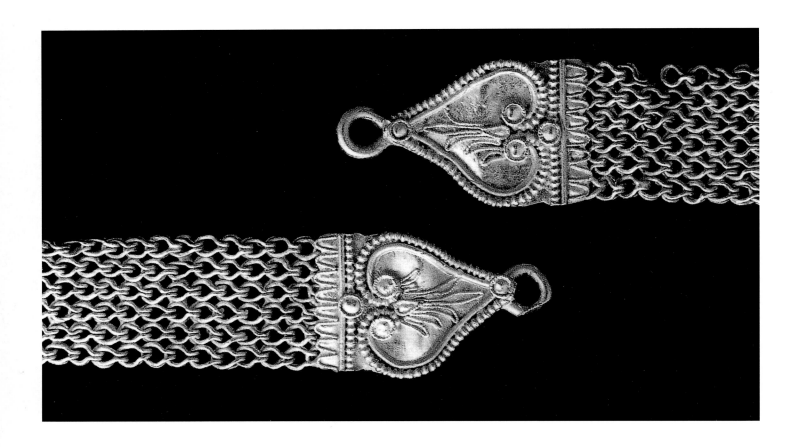

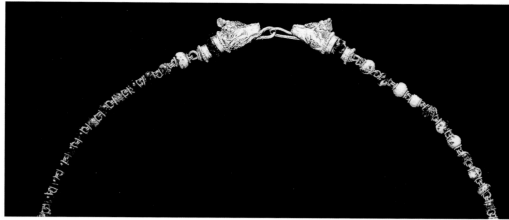

HELLENISTIC FASTENINGS

Throughout the Classical period necklaces were fastened simply by tying the cord on which the elements were strung. Around 300 B.C. some necklaces started to be fitted with a ring at one end and with a hook at the other.

This hook-and-eye fastening (*opposite above*) on a gold chain necklace terminating with goat heads comes from Cyprus, 3rd century B.C. A gold strap necklace (*opposite centre*) from Mottola, southern Italy, 3rd century B.C., has palmette-shaped terminals; note the rings through which the fastening cord was threaded. Another hook-and-eye gold chain necklace (*opposite below*) has terminals in the form of a pair of female heads, 3rd century B.C.

The illustrations on this page show a variety of fastenings (*clockwise, from top*): a gold trihemistater from Carthage, *c.* 260 B.C., depicting Kore-Persephone wearing a necklace supporting a fringe of pendants clearly tied at the back of the neck in a knot; two gold chain necklaces decorated with glass beads, terminating respectively with goat heads and dolphins and fitted with eye-and-hook fastenings, from Tarentum, 2nd century B.C.; a magnificent example of a gold chain necklace with lion head terminals and hook-and-eye fastening from southern Italy, *c.* 300 B.C.

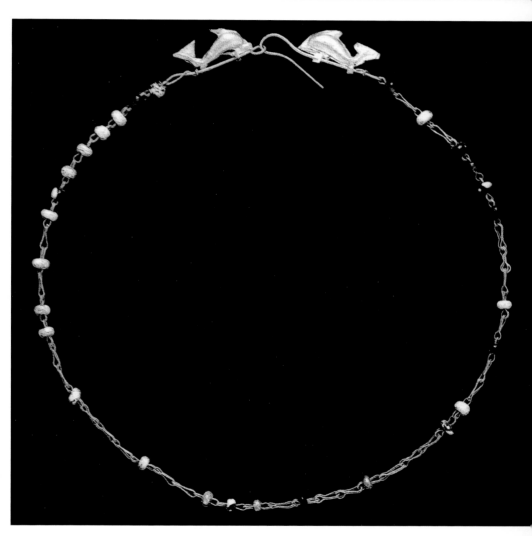

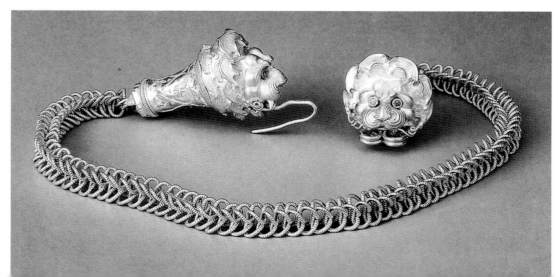

37

ROME AND BYZANTIUM I

This portrait bust (*above*) of a woman from a tomb at Palmyra (a largely autonomous oasis city on the border of the Roman province of Syria) shows the subject wearing several necklaces, graduated in length, a fashion popular throughout the Roman Empire in the 2nd and 3rd centuries A.D.

The fine Roman pierced-work of the terminal plaques *c.* A.D. 100 (*opposite above*), developed into the typical lace-like effect of Byzantine necklaces. The fine lace-like open-work decoration

of the medallion and the gem-set chain of this Byzantine emerald crystal, sapphire, pearl and gold necklace from Egypt, *c.* A.D. 600 A.D, also speaks of Roman tradition. A gold necklace from Cyprus (*opposite below*), designed as a chain of nineteen medallions decorated with scroll and cross motifs in a pierced open-work technique, dates from the Byzantine period, 7th century. Note the hook-and-eye fitting and the fretted decoration particularly popular in the Byzantine world during the 6th and 7th centuries.

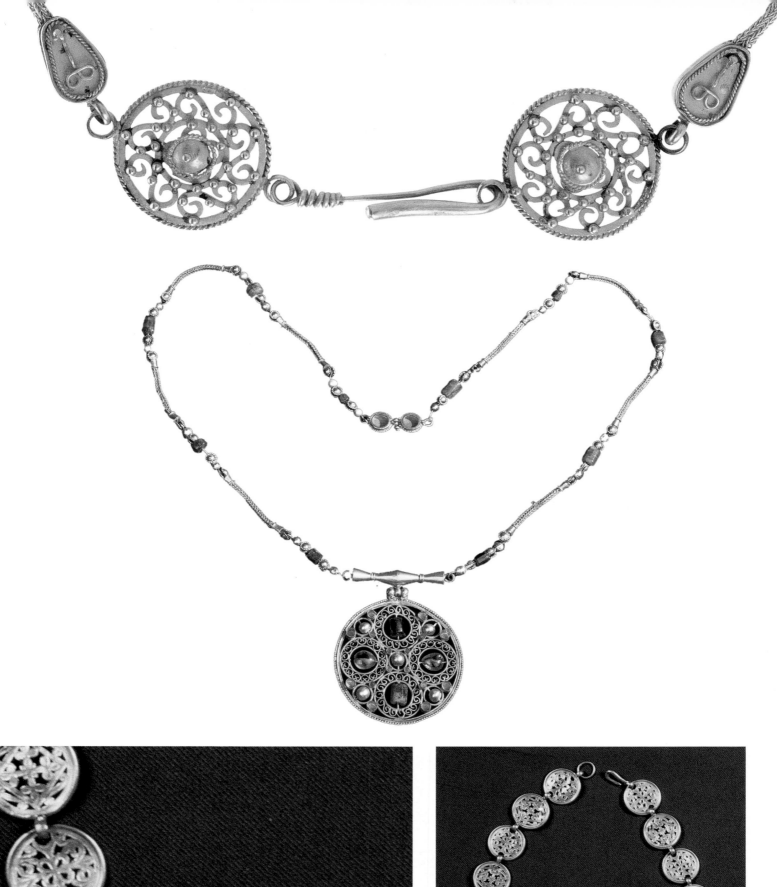

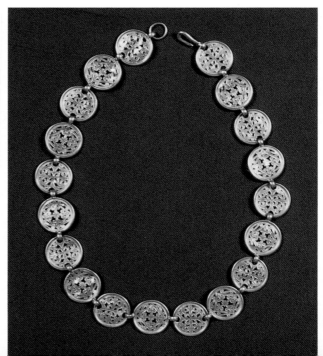

ROME AND BYZANTIUM II

Roman models remained popular throughout the Byzantine period: a gold links and cornelian bead necklace (*opposite above left*) supporting a gold disc pendant, A.D. 2nd–3rd century; a necklace of gold bar-shaped links and glass beads (*opposite above right*), A.D. 2nd-3rd century; a necklace designed as a gold chain (*opposite below left*), set with emerald beads and pearls, terminating with two gold circular plaques pierced in the shape of birds; a similar necklace (*opposite below right*), set with amethyst beads. These last two are early Byzantine examples from Cyprus, 6th–7th century.

This Roman necklace (*left*) is composed of emerald crystals and gold links, A.D. 2nd century. A wooden panel portrait (*above*) from Fayum, Egypt, shows a woman wearing types of jewels common throughout the Roman world.

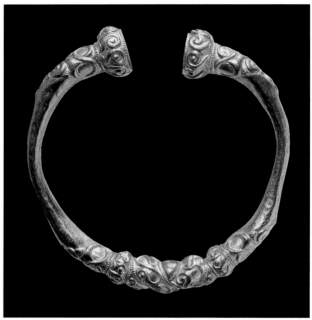

THE CELTIC TORC

From the 4th century B.C. onwards, the most typical form of torc was designed as an open ring of tubular section decorated at the two ends with variously shaped terminals.

The examples illustrated on these pages are (*clockwise from top left*): torc from the votive deposit of Snettisham, Norfolk, England, 1st century B.C., made up of eight strands of electrum, a natural alloy of gold and silver, each strand being composed of eight twisted wires decorated with cast and chased terminals; gold torc from Reinheim, Germany, 4th century B.C.; torc designed as a twisted gold bar from the deposit at Fenouillet, France, 3rd century B.C.; two torcs from Ipswich, England, with loop ends, decorated in relief, but possibly unfinished, 1st century B.C.; gold tubular torc from Mailly-le-Camp, France, late 2nd-early 1st century B.C.

A Hellenistic marble of 'The Dying Gaul' from Pergamon, second half of the 3rd century B.C., Museo Capitolino, Rome: the detail of the head shows the subject wearing a twisted torc; Classical authors mention torcs being worn by warriors, a claim partly substantiated by sculptures like this, but findings in graves have been mainly associated with female burials. The three torcs (*left*) from Ipswich, England, have loop ends, are decorated in relief, and may possibly be unfinished, 1st century B.C.

THE RENAISSANCE OF THE NECKLACE

Necklaces were especially favoured in the second half of the 15th century, as they could be successfully displayed on the skin and chest, revealed by the fashionable low *décolletage*. These necklaces were short and fitted closely to the base of the neck and, although mounted with precious gems, they were characterized by an overall simplicity in design, which consisted largely of arrangements of pearls or beads alternating in colour, sometimes supporting a pendant. Neck ornaments consisting of a ribbon suspending a large pendant were sometimes worn.

The group of Florentine portraits (*below, left to right*) illustrates this fashionable yet restrained type of neck ornament: the famous portrait of Battista Sforza, Duchess of Urbino, by Piero della Francesca, *c.* 1472 illustrates a more elaborate, though probably less common version of neck ornament; portrait of Simonetta Vespucci by Sandro Botticelli, *c.* 1470; portrait of Giovanna Tornabuoni by Domenico Ghirlandaio, 1488; portrait of a lady by Piero del Pollaiuolo, *c.* 1475.

This portrait of a young woman, by Agnolo Bronzino, *c.* 1540, illustrates the early sixteenth-century Italian fashion for wearing two necklaces, one encircling the neck and the other draped over the dress and resting around the shoulders. This particular arrangement almost certainly required the long necklace to be held in this position by means of stitching.

The portrait of Jane Seymour, third wife of King Henry VIII, painted by Hans Holbein the Younger in 1536, illustrates a fashionable form of neck ornament in English Tudor courtly circles. This consisted of a choker known as a 'carcanet' from which was often suspended a pendant; it was frequently worn together with longer jeweled chains of similar design.

The portrait of Maria Portinari, wife of Tommaso, a Medici agent living in Bruges, by Hans Memling, c. 1475, illustrates how the fashion in necklaces during the 15th century was by no means uniform throughout Europe. Neither the countries of northern Europe nor those of the Iberian peninsula adopted the simple 'Italian style' necklace, continuing to favour elaborate collars.

ARS VTINAM MORES
ANIMVM QVE EFFINGERE
POSSES PVLCHRIOR IN TER
RIS NVLLA TABELLA FORET
MCCCCLXXXVIII

LATE RENAISSANCE

This gold, polychrome enamel and diamond necklace (*opposite*), supports a figurative pendant depicting Diana the Huntress, and is set with rubies, emeralds, two small opals and pearls, probably south German, *c.* 1580–90. Note the characteristic box setting and the more jagged contours of the elements forming the necklace.

Necklaces of the period relied heavily on open-work motifs, with gemstones held mainly in box settings, as in this gold polychrome enamel necklace (*above right*) set with an emerald, rubies and pearls, probably Italian, *c.* 1600. Another example of the fashion - probably Spanish, *c.* 1600 - is this gold, polychrome enamel, diamond and *cabochon* emerald necklace (*centre right*) fringed by pearls; its central link supports a pendant of a pelican in her piety, its body a baroque pearl centred by a red enamel roundel; the clasp and six of the smaller links are later replacements.

The miniature of a necklace (*below right*) with a large cross pendant, was painted in tempera on vellum by Hans Mielich, court painter to Albrecht V of Wittelsbach, Duke of Bavaria, *c.* 1550–1560, as part of the illustrated inventory of the jewels belonging to the Duke's wife, Anna. The necklace is set alternately with diamond rosettes, characteristically portrayed in black, and four pearls; between are narrow links with lion heads; the front supports a diamond-set cross decorated with enamelled *putti* and satyrs. Note the compact outline of this necklace and the multifoil settings around the diamond rosettes which are typical features of the mid 16th century, in contrast to the open-work and jagged contours of later examples.

HIGH COLLAR, LONG NECKLACE

The examples shown in these portraits are representative of necklaces created in the second half of the 16th century; they were usually worn beneath the ruff and formed of gold, enamel and gem-set elements, in which stones and the surrounding metalwork were given equal importance: Anna of Austria, fourth wife of Philip II of Spain, by Anthonis Mor, 1570s; portrait of Catalina Micaela, daughter of Philip II of Spain, by Alonso Sánchez Coello, c. 1584; portrait of Maria de Medici, wife of Henri IV of France, by Alessandro Allori, c. 1600.

2

FROM THE MIDDLE AGES TO THE RENAISSANCE: THE NECKLACE IN DECLINE AND REVIVAL

Though great change and evolution, from the Romanesque to the Gothic, characterized almost all aspects of medieval art, the period, especially its early part, was not particularly significant in the development of the necklace. Medieval dress was not conducive to the effective display of neck ornament; the basic costume for women consisted of a long loosely fitting tunic, cropped at the neck, and worn with a mantle sometimes secured by a large brooch worn at the front of the garment.

The development of neck ornaments between 800 and 1200 is not well documented and much less is known about the jewelry of this period than that of the later Middle Ages. Very little has survived from the period and the scarce written documentation and pictorial and sculptural evidence provide insufficient detail. Among the rare references, the earliest appears in the law code of Thuringia, in central Germany, codified by Charlemagne in 802, which ordained that a daughter should inherit from her mother 'the ornaments of her neck'. These included her chains and necklaces, as well as brooches, earrings and bracelets. Despite the scanty evidence, however, it is fairly certain that the principal ornament during this period was the brooch rather than the necklace which was now entering a time of great decline.

From the 12th century until the last quarter of the 14th, neck ornaments disappear almost completely from apparel. All evidence indicates that, during this period, the

An illumination showing the wimple which made the wearing of necklaces virtually impossible, Luttrell Psalter, England, c. 1340.

choice of jewels worn at the highest levels of society both by men and women consist-ed of a variety of head ornaments, large brooches, girdles and rings, but no necklaces. This lack on the part of female adornment is not surprising, since current fashions sim-ply did not leave space for neck ornaments. The principal features of the upper part of the dress were the *barbette*, a linen band passing under the chin and drawn up over the temples, and the wimple, or *gorgette*. This was made of linen or silk and covered the neck and part of the bosom; it was sometimes tucked into the top of the gown.

The Late Medieval Necklace

During the last quarter of the 14th century, after centuries of oblivion, neck ornaments begin to reappear, eventually to rival the brooch in importance. Once again, this change in taste was brought about by a change in fashion: the introduction of tailoring and the susequent development of a bodice which revealed the figure. Another innovation, with even greater erotic appeal, which naturally came to have a direct influence on the necklace, was *décolletage*, the cutting away of the top of the robe to reveal the upper part of the bosom.

The new necklaces were conceived usually as broad collars to be worn at the base of the neck or close around the neck, as suggested by the term *carcan,* found in French records of the 1380s and 1390s, which also referred to the iron collars fastened around the necks of prisoners.

Collars were mainly of two sorts: either textile ribbons decorated with stones mounted in metal collets secured by stitching to the fabric, or made entirely of gold and precious gems. In both cases, they were fastened by means of ribbons tied at the back of the neck. Due to the lack of surviving examples, the splendour and magnificence of some collars can only be gauged from written records. Lavish collars figure prominent-ly in lists of gifts given by Philip the Good, Duke of Burgundy, in the 1390s. For exam-ple, in January 1396 he gave his wife Marguerite a collar, purchased for 2500 *livres* and set with ten balas rubies, a sapphire, and forty-four pearls supporting a great balas-ruby pendant, a certain sign of a return to lavish neck ornament.

The design of collars was fairly elaborate and probably indebted to earlier jeweled ecclesiastical collars embroidered on clerical vestments; these were formed of various jeweled elements repeated. Their decorative motifs consisted either of heraldic badges, personal devices, decorative floral and foliate elements, or a combination of all these. The most lavish examples were mounted in gold decorated with polychrome enamel-work and encrusted with precious gemstones. Not all such collars were richly jeweled; there are references to plain examples and to some mounted with semiprecious gems. Cameos, however, never seem to figure in the descriptions. As with jeweled girdles, col-lars were both broad and narrow according to fluctuations in fashion. In some instances, adjustments in length were possible in the case of collars provided with addi-tional links.

These fashionable neck ornaments served no functional purpose. They were worn purely as ornaments and to display either magnificence or, through their device, livery or allegiance. The lasting vogue for deep and revealing *décolletage,* though, ensured that such collars remained in fashion throughout most of Europe until the end of the 15th century.

The Renaissance Necklace

The transition from Gothic styles to those of the Renaissance was largely prompted by a renewed interest in the culture and arts of Ancient Greece and Rome. This new concern, however, did not extend to jewelry; there was little accurate knowledge of Greek and Roman examples, and so with the exception of cameo carving, it is difficult to describe the new Renaissance jewelry as a rebirth of the Classical tradition. It was, rather, the rediscovery of human beauty in the nude, and the recognition of man as an individual whose natural dignity springs from his qualities and merits, which were the most immediate influences on fashion and jewelry. Clothes and jewels became a means of enhancing natural human beauty, rather than overshadowing it with artificiality, thus establishing a new harmony between body, dress and ornament.

Judging from the evidence provided by Italian portraits of the period, jewelry was now being worn with some discrimination to show off the inherent beauty of the female body, and jewels to be worn directly on the body were preferred to those worn on clothes (*see pp. 44-45*). Hair ornament, rings and necklaces were especially favoured; the latter could be successfully displayed on the skin of the neck and chest, now revealed by the low *décolletage.*

The jewels of early Renaissance Italy, though lavishly mounted with precious gems, were characterized by an overall simplicity and restraint. The design of necklaces was fairly simple, consisting mainly of pearls or beads alternating in colour, sometimes supporting a pendant. These necklaces were short and fitted closely to the base of the neck; they were sometimes worn jointly with another neck ornament consisting of a long ribbon supporting a large pendant. Once again, contemporary portraiture provides the only form of visual record since no extant examples have survived, but its frequent representation indicates that this particular type was by far the most popular. But there must have been some more complex forms, as we can see from the famous portrait of Battista Sforza, Duchess of Urbino, by Piero della Francesca, *c.* 1472. This necklace consists of a wide band formed of alternating lozenge and oval enamel and gem-set plaques, the front supporting a pearl festoon and pendant (*see p. 44*).

A change in the shape of the neckline occurred around 1500 in Italy; it became less deep and therefore determined a change in necklace types and in the way in which they were worn. Higher necklines encouraged the wearing of short necklaces which encircled the bare neck, while a much longer additional ornament, either a rope of pearls or a gem-set or plain chain, was draped over the dress and rested on the shoulders (*see p. 44*).

The 'Hohenlohe Collar' in gold, polychrome enamel and sapphires, probably Burgundian, late 15th century.

This latter type appears repeatedly in contemporary portraiture arranged around the subjects' shoulders rather than just hanging down. The consistency of such treatments suggests that this was not artistic licence, but the actual manner of wearing the ornament, which may have been secured in this position by means of stitching. Such double neck ornaments, which remained in vogue in Italy until the second half of the 16th century, continued to display the general simplicity of design of the necklaces of the previous century.

The fashion for necklaces was by no means uniform throughout Renaissance Europe. During the 15th century, neither the countries of northern Europe nor those of the Iberian peninsula adopted the simple 'Italian style' necklace, continuing to favour the very elaborately jeweled and enamel collars of late medieval times. These were richly enamelled and gem-set; they incorporated entwined open-work motifs, often derived from natural models, including flowers, leaves and entwined branches and incorporating personal devices or heraldic badges. Contemporary portraiture once again compensates for the lack of extant examples and provides visual evidence for the elaborate forms of these collars. One example is shown in the portrait of Maria Portinari, wife of Tommaso, a Medici agent living in Bruges, by the Flemish artist Hans Memling, painted *c.* 1475 (*see p. 45*). It is formed of interlaced gold decorated at intervals with pearl flower-head clusters set at the centre with a gem. The magnificence of these female collars may be appreciated from an exceptionally rare and large example, probably intended to be worn by a man, known as the 'Hohenlohe Collar', after the eponymous German princely family in whose possession it has been for centuries. Probably of Burgundian origin, it dates from the third quarter of the 15th century and is formed of gold and enamel branch motifs studded with sapphires, from which is suspended a pendant in the shape of a double rose enclosing a head in profile.

The fashion for deep *décolletage* in northern Europe during the first half of the 16th century ensured the continuing popularity of the necklace. In addition, there was fashionable emphasis on the device of a matching set of jewels – the *parure* – of which the necklace was an essential component. The principal elements of the *parure* consisted of matching panels of pearls and precious stones arranged in narrow bands which assumed different names according to where they were worn. Those used to trim the wide, square neckline were called 'squares'; those attached to the headdress were referred to as 'biliments'; and those worn as chokers, fastened by means of ribbons tied at the back of the neck, were known as 'carcanets'. Sometimes pendants were suspended from the latter, which could be divided and worn as bracelets. Carcanets were frequently worn together with longer jeweled chains, often of matching design, which hung down from the neck and terminated in the cleavage. A popular form, well documented in descriptions of English Tudor courtly circles, consisted of alternating table-cut diamonds and rubies in gold settings with pairs of pearls between. One such was made for Catherine Howard and another is shown in Jane Seymour's portrait by Hans Holbein the Younger, 1536 (*see p. 48*).

By the middle of the 16th century, low square necklines had been replaced in most of Europe by high collars which gradually developed into ruffs (*see p. 48*). As the century progressed, ruffs grew so large that it is difficult to imagine how their wearers could have conveyed food to their mouths. Necklaces consequently became longer and were worn only over the dress, hanging beneath the ruff. On the whole, their design continued to rely on gemstones alternating with clusters of pearls mounted in very elaborate gold settings enriched with enamel-work. In some particularly fine examples this compact arrangement of jeweled elements was enhanced by the addition of gold plaques decorated with strap-work motifs and animal masks. Elaboration of the gold-work surrounding the gems is a distinctive feature of Renaissance jewelry, whereby gemstones and gold settings were given equal importance. It is in fact the degree of complexity of the setting and the faceting of the gemstones rather than any dramatic changes in design which differentiate early sixteenth-century neck ornaments from later ones. At the beginning of the 16th century, the settings of gems consisted of heavy gold mounts, termed *quatrefoil* or *multifoil*, a reference to the lobed decoration extending around the stone. This type of setting gradually became more complex; and the lobed planes were subdivided to form a lower part known as the 'shield'. From around 1540 this 'shield' was decorated with enamel and, from about 1550, it featured enamel strap-work decoration which then remained in vogue until the 1570s.

A design for a late sixteenth-century necklace in gold, enamel, gemstones and pearls, reproduced by Eugène Fontenay in his *Les Bijoux anciens et modernes*, Paris, 1887.

In early sixteenth-century jewels the coloured stones were either simply table-cut or polished *en cabochon* while diamonds were mainly table-cut. There is new evidence, however, in spite of the lack of extant examples, that suggests elaborate diamond faceting techniques were mastered at the Burgundian court and in Paris as early as the mid 15th century. Later on, all gemstones came to have more complex outlines. Faceted diamonds were arranged in groupings to form rosette clusters. In contemporary portraiture it is interesting to note that diamonds are shown as being black; this was simply a recognition of the fact that, in spite of their sparkle, they really did appear to be fairly dark. The reasons for this were that the minimal faceting meant that most light was reflected back, creating a mirror-like surface, and that diamonds, as was the case with all gems, were mounted in settings closed at the back and coated or foiled with black backing.

The greater uniformity, in terms of design and techniques, which characterized the production of necklaces during the second half of the 16th century was partly due to the dissemination throughout Europe of engraved printed designs. A number of similar necklace designs survive by the hands of different engravers – for instance, by Etienne Delaune from France, and also by Virgil Solis, Mattias Zundt, Erasmus Hornick, all working in Nuremberg.

Once again, due to the recyclable nature of jewelry, hardly any fine necklaces have survived from this period. We have to rely on the written evidence provided by the inventories and documents of princely families, portraiture and engraved designs to help our to our understanding and appreciation of the magnificent neck ornaments of this time. One such document is the illustrated inventory of jewelry belonging to Duchess Anna of Bavaria, painted by Hans Mielich between 1550 and 1560. It includes a fine diamond necklace typical of the elaborate style of the day (*see p. 47*).

Late sixteenth-century necklaces are characterized by a much less compact arrangement of the gemstones (*see pp. 46-47*). They differ from the heavy necklaces of the mid 16th century in their construction as a succession of delicate open-work gold motifs with jagged contours, often supporting figurative pendants. Each element is set with a central gem mounted in a high square setting with enamelled sides, in contrast to the earlier, heavier multifoil settings. These elements were often identical to those sewn on the dress. The production of this type of open-work necklace gained impetus around 1600 and seems to have flourished in Vienna and Prague, especially to cater for the Imperial court of Rudolf II. Unlike earlier Renaissance necklaces, a small number of examples have survived, possibly due to their relatively low intrinsic value, which made them less attractive for the melting down of their gold content and the recycling of the stones in new pieces.

PEARLS, PENDANTS AND SPARKLING DIAMONDS: THE NECKLACE IN THE SEVENTEENTH AND EIGHTEENTH CENTURIES

By the beginning of the 17th century a France ruled first by Henry IV and then by Louis XIII had supplanted Spain as the supreme power in European politics; she was soon also to emerge as the leader of European style. This new influence was reflected in many aspects of life and was particularly visible in the fashions of the day, which now saw a diminution of the formality which had been the mark of Spanish rule in various parts of Europe. Stiff and heavily embroidered costumes began to be abandoned in favour of less constricting garments made of flowing silken fabrics. By the early part of the century, the fashion of wearing jewels in great profusion, a characteristic of Spanish taste, had come to be regarded as vulgar. Jewels were now worn with restraint and, as during the Renaissance in Italy, were regarded as a means of enhancing feminine beauty rather than overpowering it.

The fashion for deep *décolletés* during the century encouraged the use of neck ornaments. Winged collars which bared the area around the neck replaced the large ruff of the final years of the 16th century. This had inhibited the wearing of short necklaces and the new fashion did not find favour in the puritanical Netherlands, where the ruff persisted. From the middle of the 17th century, however, ruffs were universally discarded and supplanted by 'deep scooped *décolletés*, a fashion which persisted throughout Europe until the end of the century.

The Baroque Period

Paradoxically, although the jewels of this period are often referred to as 'Baroque', their designs have none of the flamboyance, or the play of light and shade between curvilinear forms, which characterized the style in other art forms. They tend, rather, to be linear in design, flat in colour and their gemstones to be arranged in rigid, formal geometric clusters. The really distinctive feature of seventeenth-century jewelry is the greater emphasis given to faceted gemstones. These were beginning to become the focus of the jewel, to the detriment of elaborate enamelled work and diminution in importance of the work of goldsmiths. This was a result both of the greater availability of precious gemstones on the European market, due to the growth of trade with the East, and of improvements in lapidary techniques. The spirit of the burgeoning Oriental trade is epitomized by the figure of the French traveller, businessman, gem-dealer and connoisseur Jean-Baptiste Tavernier (1605–89), who undertook numerous voyages to Persia and India with the purpose of acquiring gemstones, primarily diamonds, which were then being extensively mined from the alluvial deposits of the Deccan region in Southern India. At the same time, advances in knowledge of refraction and the principles of analytical geometry stimulated progress in the faceting and polishing of diamonds in the traditional centres of Antwerp, Amsterdam and Paris, where diamond-cutters had been established since the mid 17th century. A growing sophistication in the fashioning of diamonds became apparent at this time, with the gradual evolution from the basic point-and-table cut to the brilliant.

Extant examples of early seventeenth-century necklaces are extremely rare. The types fashionable in the latter part of the 16th century, designed as successions of delicate open-work gold motifs, remained in vogue for the first decades of the new century. They did, however, differ from late Renaissance models in the greater emphasis given to faceted gemstones arranged in large formal clusters. These the stones were set close to one another, displacing the gold- and enamel-work which had been such a feature of sixteenth-century jewelry.

The increased emphasis on the faceted gem also encouraged the fashion for wearing lines of gemstones of substantial size around the neck. These were mounted in very plain closed collets, sometimes embellished with enamel; they may be regarded as the forerunners of the characteristic eighteenth-century *rivière* necklaces. It was only in the second half of the 17th century, however, that distinctively new designs for neck ornaments made their appearance in the form of short necklaces of ribbon-bow motifs (*see p. 65*). This motif had never been exploited in jewelry design before and it was most likely inspired by the silk or velvet ribbon bows associated with the display of jewels since the early 1600s, when they were used to fasten necklaces, suspend pearl drops on earrings and support pendants or lockets pinned on to the corsage. Necklaces of this type frequently featured polychrome painted enamel decoration, a technique developed in the early decades of the century by the French jeweler, Jean Toutin (1578–1640), to produce opaque white or pale blue backgrounds with black decoration or vice versa. A fine and rare surviving example of this type is a necklace dating from the 1660s, in blue and white opaque enamel and supporting a sapphire bead and pearl drop, now in the collection of the Victoria & Albert Museum in London. Lush naturalistic floral decoration was another great design innovation of the second half of the 17th century. Such decoration often featured on the reverse of necklaces in the form of realistic renderings of tulips, lilies, roses and fritillaries, the result of a great interest at the time in the study of botany generated by the importing of exotic species from the East. Fine examples of necklaces incorporating bow and floral motifs feature in *Ouvrages d'Orfèvrerie*, published in 1663 by the French jeweler, Gilles Légaré (*see p. 65*).

Undoubtedly, though, the most fashionable form of neck ornament throughout the century was the pearl necklace (*see pp. 66-67*). Its popularity is confirmed by its ubiquitous presence in contemporary society portraits – notably in the work of Van Dyck (1599–1641) – and by numerous written sources. Pearls could be threaded into short chokers, multiple-rowed necklaces or long ropes. Such strings sometimes supported large gem-set pendants or fringes of pear-shaped pearl drops. A common feature of all these necklaces was that they were fastened by means of a ribbon tie, as can be seen in Arnold Lulls' coloured designs on vellum of court jewelry for James I of England, *c.* 1605. Here, two necklaces, formed of 47 pearls graduated in size from approximately 9 mm to 16 mm in diameter, are tied with red ribbons, one supporting a large enamel and gem-set pendant with a pearl drop. By the end of the century, though, longer multi-strand examples appeared with fastenings of gem-set clasps.

Pearls were already valued for their size, regular shape, colour and orient, or sheen, and fine examples from the Persian Gulf and Ceylon were keenly sought after and highly prized. In the first sixty years of the century their price tripled, hardly surprising given the insatiable demand of the time. Contemporary portraiture reveals the profusion in which pearls were worn and also the prevalence of very large specimens. It is likely, however, that not all pearls worn at this time were natural; the great quantities used everywhere in Europe created a demand for imitations. Venice was already an established centre for the manufacture of pearl simulants and, from the 17th century onwards, France started to compete in this market, largely as a result of the bead-maker Jaquin patenting an alternative method of fashioning pearl simulants. This consisted of coating the inside of blown glass spheres with a mixture of ground fish scales and varnish and then filling them with wax for strength and weight.

Rococo to Neoclassicism

The death of Louis XIV of France in 1715 signalled the end of the opulence and formality which had marked the spirit of the court at Versailles and influenced all the arts, both in France and elsewhere in Europe. The Regency and the eventual coming of age of Louis XV heralded an era characterized by a new spirit of light-heartedness and elegance. This new *esprit* spread rapidly from France to the rest of Europe, expressing itself most notably in the body of art and design generally designated as Rococo. The lightness, asymmetry, pale palette and general gaiety of this movement were in distinct contrast to the gravitas of High Baroque. In terms of jewelry, this freshness was translated into graceful asymmetric and fluid designs which remained in vogue until the 1770s, when the seriousness of Neoclassicism began to assert itself in the form of jewels made up of plain geometrical elements, with a prevalence of oval and *marquise* shapes arranged symmetrically in designs derived from Classical models.

For part of the 18th century, however, ladies' fashion was enlivened by extreme and varied eccentricities. In the 1740s, with the help of the supporting structure of the *panier*, the skirt was extended sideways up to a distance of 5 metres. This vogue caused no small inconvenience: it became impossible for two ladies to pass through a door side by side or even sit on the same sofa. In the 1770s towering hairstyles reached nearly a metre in height, as the natural hair, with the addition of false attachments, was drawn over a pad or a wire fame, the whole creation then plastered with pomatum and covered with white powder. There was, however, one constant feature in eighteenth-century fashion: the deep *décolleté*, which was common to both formal and informal garments, making the necklace one of the most important forms of adornment. In some instances, however, mainly in the case of day wear, the deep *décolleté* was reduced by a variety of expedients. A neckerchief, consisting of a square of silk or muslin, might be draped around the neck, or a 'modesty piece' or 'tucker' could serve as trimming along the edge of the bodice and conceal the lower part of the *décolletage*. Such, however, did nothing to reduce the importance of the necklace, as this was short and worn high on the neck. Contemporary portraiture repeatedly shows a very high position, although it is doubtful whether the necklaces could have been worn there for any length of time without becoming excessively constricting. This mode was clearly meant to emphasize the length and elegance of the wearer's neck. An elongated, swan-like neck was the likely aspiration of most sitters and contemporary painters were probably keen to satisfy it. Necklaces, together with earrings, were certainly the most popular form of jeweled ornament, especially those mounted with diamonds, the ultimate status symbol for every woman of means.

The design of these short necklaces was a close reflection of the general trends in the decorative arts of the time. In the first half of the century they were formed of interlaced ribbons entwined with floral and foliate motifs whose intricate design conveyed a distinctly lace-like quality. Less intricate necklaces with ornaments arranged in increasingly regular and ordered forms became fashionable in the third quarter of the century as a reflection of Neoclassical design. These often featured successions of gemstone clusters forming florets or foliate motifs.

The first distinct type of eighteenth-century necklace consisted of an articulated open-work band of varying width set with a variety of gemstones (*see pp. 68-69*). This basic form could be enriched by the addition of a central pendant either in the shape of a ribbon bow or a cross. Alternatively, it could support a pendant designed as a pear-shaped drop or an elaborate combination of ribbon bow and drops which matched the *pendeloque* and *girandole* design of earrings. The most elaborate version of this type of necklace was known as the *esclavage*, which consisted of the basic open-work band embellished with single or multiple central festoons, often enriched with pendants (*see pp. 70-71, 72-73*). All these additional elements could be detached from the basic band by means of a hook-and-eye device, making this type of neck ornament particularly versatile. These necklaces were worn either directly on the skin or backed by black velvet or other coloured fabric which matched the dress. In most cases, they were fastened at the back by ribbons attached to circular or D-shaped metal loops to ensure a perfect fit around the neck. This was achieved by adjusting the ribbons at the back as necessary. Contemporary portraiture frequently shows the ribbon at the back knotted into a very large bow, thus transforming a practical device into a prominent decorative feature. The length of such necklaces was variable. Some encircled the entire neck, while others restricted their decorative elements to the front, with the sides and back completed by ribbons. The reason for this peculiarity is obviously related to cost; for those who could not afford a full necklace, these shortened versions provided a good compromise.

One of the most lavish and notorious *esclavage* necklaces was that commissioned by Louis XV for his mistress Madame du Barry for the sum of 1,600,000 *livres,* which was later to provoke a scandal involving Marie Antoinette. Louis XV died before the

A mid eighteenth-century portrait of Charlotte, Countess of Abingdon, showing the short, high necklace which emphasized the elegance of the neck, studio of Nathaniel Dance.

A gold, silver, ruby and diamond
necklace with matching pendent
earrings, Palermo, 1767.

necklace was completed and paid for; the court jewelers, Böhmer and Bassenge, then tried unsuccessfully to sell it to Louis XVI. Eventually a plot to steal the necklace was formulated by the Comtesse de la Motte, who convinced the innocent Cardinal de Rohan that the Queen wished to purchase it without the King's knowledge. The Cardinal bought the piece supposedly on the Queen's behalf, only to have the necklace removed from his possession and shipped to England where it was broken up. When this story finally reached the public it was generally believed that the Queen had some complicity in the matter – a belief which undoubtedly helped to reinforce the widespread discontent with the monarchy.

Another type of necklace fashionable in the 18th century was the *rivière*. Designed as a simple line of gemstones, often graduated in size from the centre and mounted in plain collets, it was generally strung on silk in the early part of the century, but later examples have the collets connected to each other by small circular metal links. When strung, the closed collets were furnished on the underside with two parallel tubes through which threads were passed. The stones were thus secured by a double row of threads; if one broke, the other held the necklace together. These *rivières* were often embellished at the front with a pear-shaped drop set in cruciform shape with matching stones, which was the ideal way of supporting and offsetting a gemstone – usually a diamond – of particularly large size. By the last quarter of the century the diamond *rivière* had become *the* fashionable neck ornament.

The diamond was undoubtedly the gemstone *par excellence* of the 18th century. Throughout the century every woman of means aspired to the ownership of a diamond rose or a brilliant-cut diamond necklace, although from about 1760 onwards coloured gemstones became increasingly fashionable. The great popularity of diamonds was due to a combination of factors. The first and most important was the opening of diamond mines at Minas Gerais in Brazil in 1723, just as the Indian mines of Golconda were being exhausted. This led to an increased availability of rough diamonds on the market to be faceted with the recently improved cutting techniques. During the last decade of the 17th century the brilliant-cut had been devised – a cut that enhanced the optical properties of diamonds and enabled the stone to reflect light and sparkle. Thirdly, improved domestic candle lighting meant that more social occasions, such as balls, operas and masquerades, could be held at night, when jewels set with diamonds would catch and reflect light.

Large diamonds were especially coveted and often suspended at the front of *rivières*. Marie Leczinska, the queen of Louis XV, had a diamond band necklace made in 1739 to suspend the historic Sancy diamond of 55.23 carats. She wore this necklace some eight years later when she sat for her portrait by Carle van Loo, now in the collection of the palace of Versailles.

During the course of the second half of the century coloured stones such as emeralds, sapphires and especially rubies were used more frequently in both necklaces to be worn tight round the neck and in those *en esclavage* (*see pp. 74-75*). Lemon-yellow chrysoberyls and orange-pink topazes from Brazil also became fashionable in necklaces to be worn in the evening, although diamonds continued to be preferred for *rivières* to be worn in candle-light and on grand formal occasions. Colourless glass pastes, white topaz and rock crystal were extensively employed as diamond simulants. Beautifully designed necklaces skilfully set in silver with multicoloured glass pastes variously foiled to enhance their colour and faceted to fit the mounts, were socially acceptable even among the aristocracy, who sometimes found it advisable to wear substitutes rather than the real thing (*see pp. 76-77*).

Necklaces worn during the day were often made of less precious materials such as garnets, cornelians, foiled rock crystals and agates, mounted simply in gold collets and connected in *rivières*. This differentiation between day-time and night-time jewels was without precedent in the history of jewelry and was largely prompted by the improvements in candle lighting mentioned above. Day-time necklaces often had a better chance of surviving unaltered to the present day, since their low intrinsic value made them less likely to be dismantled and remodelled. Indeed, their survival has been of paramount importance in the reconstruction of the design of eighteenth-century necklaces, as their shapes and types of fastenings closely imitated the more costly jeweled examples, many of which are irrevocably lost.

Setting and mounting techniques made considerable progress during the century (*see pp. 78-79*). At its beginning, the seventeenth-century fashion for opulent enamel-work to the back of jewels had completely disappeared. However, necklaces set in gold with relatively few or small gemstones and decorated on the reverse with elaborate engravings of floral and foliate motifs – a development of seventeenth-century enamel decoration – were still being produced in the first decades of the new century, especially in Spain and Portugal, which had been slower to accept the new fashions than other European countries and were still relatively conservative in taste.

Top The design of the so-called 'Queen's Necklace', a lavish diamond *esclavage* commissioned by Louis XV from Böhmer and Bassenge, but only completed after the king's death in 1774.

Above A gold, silver and paste necklace with matching *pendeloque* earrings, Portuguese, late 18th century.

As soon as diamonds became fashionable, silver mounts closed at the back became the most popular form of setting, while gold continued to be used for coloured gems. Silver naturally complemented the colour of diamonds, and closed settings allowed jewelers to impart to the gems delicate pastel hues by lining the collet with coloured foils. The technique of foiling also facilitated the difficult task of matching coloured gemstones, such as rubies, emeralds and topazes, at a time when supply was relatively limited and of varying quality. One disadvantage of using silver for setting stones was that a large quantity of metal was needed to keep the gems in place. This resulted in ornaments which were often heavy and cumbersome, and which tarnished quickly, causing discolouring to skin and clothing. The gold lining which was sometimes applied to the back of the mounts to eliminate this inconvenience made the jewels even heavier to wear. Small gems were often set close to each other in a tight paved effect, while larger specimens were mounted in single collets.

Towards the end of the century, especially in jewelry constructed with brilliant-cut diamonds, in which the older rose-cut frequently played a subsidiary role, the gems were given greater depth and sparkle by being mounted in open collets that allowed light to reflect and refract through the stones. Open settings were certainly not a new invention – written evidence confirms that jewels mounted with diamonds in this way were being created in England as early as 1702. However, it is unlikely that the open setting technique was taken up in any major way by the jewelry trade until the last quarter of the century.

Another feature of late eighteenth-century gem setting was the decoration of the rim of the collet with a beaded effect, which imparted a sense of lightness to the jewel. As mentioned above, the most common form of necklace fastening throughout the century consisted of a ribbon threaded through two D-shaped loops secured to the two ends of the ornament. Metal clasps existed but were not as popular as the former type, since they could not easily secure heavy ornaments. Metal spring clasps increased in popularity towards the end of the century, when the fashion for wide-band necklaces, to be worn tight on the neck, started to decline in favour of much simpler and lighter *rivières* of single gems or simple floral clusters (*see p. 80*).

A large amount of eighteenth-century French jewels were eventually to end up in England, where jewelers, in particular Philip Rundell, were quick to purchase them at relatively low prices from the French aristocrats who had fled during the Revolution. Some were sold at public auction by James Christie and described as the property of 'An Emigrant of Fashion' or a 'Foreigner of Rank'. The jewels of Madame du Barry, former mistress of Louis XV, were auctioned on 19 February 1795. The immediate consequence of this influx of jewelry was a depression in price not only on the British market but across Europe. A more lasting effect, though, was an irretrievable loss to the history of jewelry design, since most of these ornaments were broken up and the gems remounted or stored for future needs. This explains why so few eighteenth-century necklaces of high intrinsic value have survived in their original form.

RIBBONS AND BOWS

This necklace (*above*) is a fine example of gold ribbon-bow design of the 1660s, probably French. It is decorated in opaque blue, white and black painted enamel, set with table-cut diamonds, supporting a rather coarse sapphire bead and pearl drop; this latter feature could be a subsequent addition.

Another design innovation of the second half of the 17th century was naturalistic floral decoration; this featured frequently on the reverse of the necklace elements (*left*) illustrated in the engraved designs published in 1663 by French jeweler Gilles Légaré.

THE UBIQUITOUS PEARL

The pearl necklace was a ubiquitous presence in seventeenth-century society portraits: Anne of Denmark, wife of James I of England, by Marcus Gheeraerts, *c.* 1605–1610, is shown (*below*) wearing a double strand of pearls, supporting a pear-shaped faceted gemstone on a black ribbon bow at the front. Dorothy, Lady Dacre, by Van Dyck, *c.* 1633; the subject is depicted with a single strand of large pearls and pendant earrings mounted with perfectly matched pear-shaped drop pearls often described as *union d'excellence*, due to their rarity and beauty.

This group portrait (*left*) of the Regentesses of the Orphanage in Amsterdam, by Adriaen Backer, 1683, shows all the subjects wearing single-strand pearl necklaces, the height of fashion throughout Europe in the 17th century.

Henrietta Maria, wife of Charles I of England, painted by Van Dyck, *c*. 1639, is shown wearing a single-strand pearl necklace. This portrait of Elizabeth of Bohemia, daughter of James I of England and Anne of Denmark, by the studio of Michiel van Miereveld, *c*. 1615–20, shows the sitter wearing a pearl necklace supporting a fringe of exceptionally large pear-shaped drops.

OPEN-WORK BANDS

The deep *décolleté* was a dominant feature in eighteenth-century fashion; it was common to both formal and informal garments, making the necklace together with long pendant earrings one of the most important forms of personal adornment. Necklaces of the time were short and worn high on the neck. Contemporary portraiture frequently shows the ribbon at the back knotted into a very large bow, thus transforming a practical device into a prominent decorative feature. This is clearly illustrated (*above left*) in the portrait of a lady, said to be Mrs Casberd, painted by Thomas Gainsborough, *c.* 1765; the delicate open-work necklace is positioned very high and secured at the back by means of a very decorative ribbon-bow knot. Augusta, Princess of Wales, whose son became George III on the death of his grandfather George II in 1760, in a portrait (*above right*) by the studio of Jean-Baptiste Van Loo, *c.* 1745; she is depicted wearing the fashionable necklace of the time, formed of a delicate interlaced open-work band. The front supports a ribbon bow and pear-shaped drop motif and is closely set with faceted gemstones. She is also wearing large *pendeloque* earrings which match the design of the necklace pendant and an elegant *aigrette* in her hair.

This portrait of the Infanta Maria Louisa (*above*), painted by Anton Raphael Mengs in 1764–65, shows the sitter wearing a necklace with a pear-shaped drop at the front, mounted with coloured gems backed by black material. She is wearing matching *girandole* earrings and an *aigrette* in her hair. Heinrich-Carl Brandt's portrait (*right*) of Caroline Felizitas Fürstin of Nassau-Usingen, probably painted in the 1760s, emphasizes the fine diamond-set necklace with bow and pear-shaped drop pendant backed by azure-coloured silk to match the small plumes in the sitter's hair; diamond *girandole* earrings and an *aigrette* complete the picture.

EN ESCLAVAGE

The typical eighteenth-century necklace consisted of an articulated open-work band of floral, foliate or ribbon design, with a variety of gemstones. This could be embellished with a central decorative motif: a bow, a pear-shaped drop, or an elaborate *girandole* pendant. The most elaborate version was the *esclavage*, of which the open-work band might also have one or more central festoons, often with pendants.

This Sicilian ruby and diamond necklace (*below*), second half of the 18th century, has matching pendant earrings. Typically, its design includes a ribbon bow and a *girandole* pendant, matching the earrings. A necklace of similar design (*opposite left*), with an *esclavage* motif, is worn by Marie-Antoinette in this portrait by François-Hubert Drouais, *c.* 1750; Marie-Amélie of Bavaria, portrayed by Raphael Mengs, *c.* 1760, is shown wearing a necklace with central bow motif applied on a ribbon of contrasting colour. The sitter in this portrait (*left*), engraved by Frye, *c.* 1760, is wearing an *esclavage* in the form of a string of pearls supporting seven festoons of pearls of graduated length, the longest with a large pear-shaped pearl drop; the pearls are worn on a ruched ribbon decorated at the front with a bow motif.

HIGH FASHION IN THE 18TH CENTURY

Two designs for *esclavage* necklaces (*opposite*): the example by
Pouget (*above*), 1762, is characterized by a simple ribbon band
supporting multiple festoons of elaborate floral and foliate
motifs. In the design *below* a band of foliate motifs supports a
single festoon, typically decorated with a bow and cruciform
pendant. The D-shaped terminal loops were designed to provide
a suitable attachment for the ribbon which was the customary
fastening for necklaces throughout the century. In the detail of
the portrait of Miss Mary Edwards (1705–43) by William
Hogarth (*below*), the sitter wears an elaborate neck ornament,
consisting of a row of pearls supporting an elaborate *esclavage*
of diamonds with a central ribbon-bow motif and a cruciform
pendant. The detail of a portrait of Mary, Countess of
Macclesfield, by Francis Coates, exhibited at the Society of
Artists in 1763 (*right*), shows the countess wearing a fashionable
necklace *en esclavage* high on the neck; it covers her deep *decolleté*
with several gem-set festoons. She wears a pair of *girandole*
earrings, while her elaborate hairstyle is embellished with an
intricate jewel of floral and foliate design.

AN EIGHTEENTH-CENTURY *PARURE*

This gold and foiled garnet *parure*, dating from the third quarter of the 18th century, includes an *esclavage* necklace, a pair of *pendeloque* earrings and two hair ornaments. The necklace is designed as an open-work band of floral and ribbon motifs, supporting a similarly designed detachable festoon with cruciform pendant. The reverse of the jewels (*below*) clearly shows that the festoon and the cruciform pendant are attached to the main part of the necklace by hook-and-eye devices which allow the necklace to be worn in a reduced form on less formal occasions. The fittings on the backs of the earrings are later alterations, but it is rare to find a complete and almost perfect set of jewels of the period still cased in their original fitted box. The irregular shape of the case (*opposite*) and the ruffled silk lining provide the ideal backdrop for the jewels and are a wonderful expression of Rococo light-heartedness.

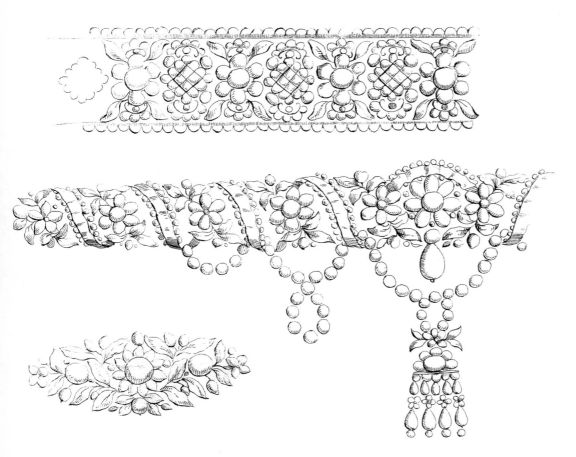

ROCOCO GARLANDS

Leaf and flower forms arranged as garlands, entwined with ribbons, bow motifs, pear-shaped drops and cruciform pendants, were a constant feature in the design of necklaces in the mid 18th century. Illustrated on this page (*top to foot of page*) are: a silver and opaline paste necklace, designed as a ribbon of foliate motifs supporting a bow and pear-shaped drop, probably French, *c.* 1860; two elaborate engraved designs for necklaces by Pouget, 1762, one supporting a tassel-shaped drop *en esclavage*; north European necklace set with rose and table-cut diamonds designed as a garland of flowers tied with ribbon-bow motifs, *c.* 1875; the central plaque is in the shape of a bird perched on a branch of leaves. Two engraved designs (*opposite*) for necklaces of floral and ribbon design, also by Pouget, 1762; the second example has a bold ribbon-bow motif in the centre. Another design for a necklace of intricate foliate scroll motifs supporting a cruciform pendant (*opposite*); this Italian example has a rather tight and compact composition which, with the formal cruciform pendant, suggests an earlier date.

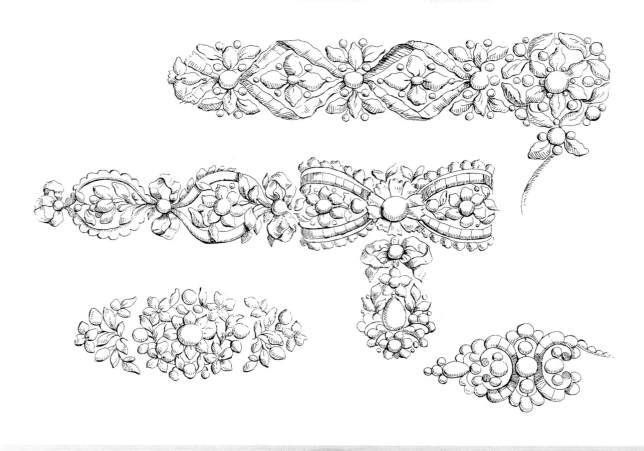

THE NEOCLASSICAL NECKLACE

This silver, aquamarine and diamond necklace
(*left*), shown front and reverse, is probably
English, late 18th century. The simple design,
composed of a line of oval gemstone clusters, is
typical of the last decades of the century, when
jewelry started to adopt simpler, geometrical
shapes in contrast to the flowery designs of
the earlier part of the century. The reverse
of the necklace shows the closed settings which
allowed jewelers to enhance, alter or match the
colour of the gemstones by lining the collets
with coloured foils, a practice which lasted until
the century's closing years.

An earlier English necklace (*opposite*), *c.* 1760, in
gold and foiled garnet has a floral and foliate
design. The pear-shaped drop on the ribbon-
bow surmount, the garnet and the D-shaped
terminals for the ribbon make this necklace a
typical example of its date; the fitted case echoes
the design of the necklace. A later, silver and
topaz necklace (*opposite below*), *c.* 1870, probably
Portuguese, has a band of flowerhead clusters
alternating with C-shaped links. Note how the
gemstones are cut *en calibré* to fit the mount
perfectly. As was customary at the time, they are
foiled to enhance their colour and mounted in
closed settings.

THE SIMPLE *RIVIÈRE*

Both these necklaces (*above*) are probably English, *c.* 1800; the first is designed as a chain of rosette-shaped clusters set with foiled garnets, while the second is set with multicoloured foiled gemstones. The foiled garnet necklace (*below*), again probably English, late 18th century, is designed as a *rivière* of paired oval-shaped, rose-cut stones. Note the metal spring clasp concealed in the collet of the single garnet at the back; such clasps increased in popularity towards the end of the century, when the fashion for wide-band necklaces, worn tight on the neck, declined in favour of *rivières* of single gems or simple floral clusters.

VARIETY AND OPULENCE:
THE NECKLACE IN THE NINETEENTH
CENTURY

When the new republican ideals of the Revolution of 1789 swept away the Ancien Régime, it was all-change in France: habits, lifestyles, government, religion and calendar. Even the rest of Europe, though not immediately involved in this upheaval, nevertheless felt its effects. Paris had been the undisputed centre of jewelry manufacture; the output of fine jewelry design now came to a temporary halt, as ostentatious adornment was felt to conflict with the revolutionary principles of the new régime. Moreover, many French aristocrats, the traditional patrons of the jewelers, had fled the country, taking their valuables to sell abroad and thus depriving the jewelry trade of both patrons and precious materials – old jewels for restyling and new imported bullion and gemstones.

Like all great social upheavals, the French Revolution also had a profound effect on fashion. Suddenly, there were no more brocaded gowns, no more wigs or powdered hair, no more *paniers*, bustles or corsets. Simplicity was the keynote. Women started to wear high-waisted long muslin or calico garments, usually characterized by deep and revealing *décolleté* and devoid of superfluous ornamentation. These tunic-like dresses, inspired by those of Ancient Greece, were light and transparent, and sometimes dampened so that they clung to the body in imitation of those worn by pagan goddesses in ancient statuary. This attempt to emulate Classical simplicity meant that there was hardly any differentiation between day-time wear and full evening dress. The style spread very rapidly and showed little variation across Europe.

The Bridging Years, 1795–1815

The establishment of the Directoire in 1795 heralded a slow return to more settled trading conditions in France. Supplies of luxury materials were gradually restored and the jewelry trade started to recover. Just as the new style in dress showed a simplicity inspired by Classical antiquity, so did the jewels which complemented it. They were light and flat, their designs linear and geometrical, rather than flowery and intricate (*see p. 97*). They were often conceived as a repetition of similar motifs with connecting elements formed of fine chains or stylized scroll-work, and included motifs such as Greek key, acanthus and laurel leaves. Cameos and intaglios were used extensively, frequently featuring characters from Greek and Roman mythology.

As deep *décolleté* was the fashion even for day-time dress, it is not surprising that necklaces were a favoured form of ornament. They were mainly short and designed to decorate the base of the neck. There were two main types. The first included *rivières* of stones in individual collets, with or without drops, and necklaces formed of a succession of clusters set with smaller stones. The second and commonest type consisted of a central motif connected by multiple festoons of fine gold chains to similar elements, often graduated in size. Early examples of this type are formed of a single element, worn at the front, on gold chains. This style could also be extended in length and worn

A gold and shell cameo necklace, possibly Italian, *c.* 1805.

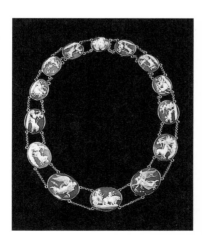

over one shoulder and under the other in a fashion said to have been inspired by the military practice of wearing a sash across the chest of the tunic. The French named this necklace *sautoir* and this word has been used ever since to describe long neck ornaments.

Just as day-time dress did not differ in form from evening wear (except for the choice of material – cotton for the day and silk for the evening) so the overall design of necklaces remained the same for all occasions (*see pp. 102-103*). The materials, however, differed: semiprecious stones for the day and sumptuous gems for the evening. The selection of materials for day-wear necklaces was wide-ranging. It included cameos carved either in shell or in hardstone and intaglios depicting subjects mainly inspired by antiquity. For example, the Frankfurt edition of the *Journal des Dames* noted in 1805 that the latest cameo necklaces were mounted with complete sets of the Roman emperors, from Caesar to Nero and from Nero to Constantine. Other necklaces featured mosaic plaques, which were either formed of inlays of hardstone depicting naturalistic subjects, commonly known as Florentine mosaics, or were made of minute glass tesserae often depicting archaeological views, known as Roman mosaics or micromosaics. Among hardstones, coral, lapis lazuli and malachite were not uncommon, as well as agates in all their varieties, including bloodstone, jasper, banded and moss agate. When gemstones did not feature, jewelers availed themselves of the decorative potential of polychrome enamels. Strings of gemstone beads and seed pearls provided an alternative to gold chains.

All these materials were invariably mounted in very thin sheet gold, making the necklaces very light. While this lightness undoubtedly complemented the flimsiness of contemporary dress, it was also a response to the scarcity of imported precious materials which affected France especially, but was felt to a lesser degree by the rest of Europe. Characteristically, gems were held in open or closed collets either rubbed over or pinched around their girdles. One novelty was that necklaces were now being fastened by metal spring clasps rather than tied at the back with ribbons threaded through metal loops, as had been common up to the end of the 18th century.

Compared with the large numbers of surviving necklaces mounted with less precious materials, there are very few examples of this period mounted with precious gemstones (*see pp. 100-101*). Gems of high intrinsic value were frequently removed from their mounts and reset at a later stage in more up-to-date ornaments. The few surviving examples, and extensive pictorial evidence, confirm that the overall design of these precious necklaces conformed to the two main types mentioned above: those designed as *rivières* and those formed of variously shaped elements connected by festoon motifs. The principal innovation in the production of *rivières* was in the setting, their design continuing to reflect eighteenth-century styles. The stones, mainly diamonds, were mounted in open collet settings, which allowed light to penetrate the back of the gem for the first time and displayed the diamonds' optical qualities to the best advantage. Another novelty was the connection of each collet by metal links rather than the previously common threading.

The second type of necklace, of clusters connected by chains of precious gemstones, was particularly favoured at the court of Napoleon (*see pp. 98-99*). Its design – Classical in inspiration but opulent in interpretation – accurately reflected the aspirations of the newly-established imperial court; its splendour was a symbol of prestige and national confidence. One of the finest surviving necklaces of the time, mounted with clusters of emeralds and diamonds, was commissioned most probably from the Parisian jeweler Nitot, founder of the firm of Chaumet, and given as a wedding gift by Napoleon to his adoptive daughter, Stéphanie de Beauharnais, on the occasion of her marriage to the Grand Duke of Baden in 1806. Characteristically, its overall design is similar to those mounted with less precious materials, but emerald and diamond clusters replace cameos or mosaics, with chains of alternating emeralds and diamonds instead of gold. A feature of such extravagant creations is that the large coloured gemstones as well as the diamonds were usually mounted in open settings – the norm in the decades to follow.

A number of lavishly set diamond *rivières* survive in Britain; these are perhaps an indication of the preference for more traditional design in a country where diamonds were relatively more abundant than in the rest of Europe. British stone merchants in fact managed to overcome the restrictions of the naval blockade decreed by Napoleon in 1806 by dealing directly with Brazil, thus bypassing the normal trade route via Portugal. It was also around this time that British jewelry firms, such as Rundell, Bridge & Rundell of London, began mounting jewels with the many gems acquired very cheaply from French *émigrés* who had fled the Revolution.

Old Designs, New Materials, 1815–40

The efforts of the European heads of state to reorganize the political map of Europe at the Congress of Vienna in 1815 were soon reflected in all forms of the applied arts. Fashion gradually reverted to a silhouette which recalled the complexity and elaboration of the 18th century in both dress and hairstyles. By 1820 the waistline had dropped to position corresponding to the natural one; skirts were flared in bell-shaped form and sleeves had puffed out. Evening dress was characterized by a straight-across, off-the-shoulder *décolleté*, adorned with elaborate necklaces. Often, during the day, the *décolletage* was concealed by ruffs of Elizabethan inspiration or by wide, flat *pélerine* collars.

Necklaces were short, but still long enough to rest on the collar bones and adorn the wide area left bare by the *décolleté*. Necklace designs, following contemporary fashion, were reminiscent of eighteenth-century models. Typically, they consisted either of a *rivière* of gems or of gemstone clusters supporting detachable pendants in a variety of interpretations of *girandole*, *pendeloque* and cross motifs. These could also be worn as brooches or *devants-de-corsages*. At times, the gem-set chain was replaced by skeins of variously worked gold chains, one of the many instances of revivalism in the century. If in terms of design these necklaces recall the 18th century, in materials they could not be more different. Diamonds mounted in silver, a staple ingredient of eighteenth-century necklaces, were replaced by colourful gemstones and gold (*see pp. 106-107*). Violet amethysts, light-blue aquamarines, golden chrysoberyls, pale-green peridot, yellow citrines and pink topazes were used for these creations, along with emeralds and rubies in the most lavish and expensive examples. Typical features of such necklaces are their light mounts made of gold filigree or *cannetille*, a technique of working fine gold wires into lace-work patterns, named after a type of embroidery in very fine gold and silver thread. Scarcity of gold bullion was another reason for light, fine work.

The strong emphasis on colour was further underlined by the technique of 'foiling' each coloured gem. This involved placing a thin reflective metal sheet between the closed mount and the gemstone. Often these foils were of the same hue as the stone, so that its colour was intensified. Furthermore, this technique allowed jewelers to use gemstones of uneven colour in the same piece by achieving an artificial match through the coloured foil. This was an advantage at a time when good colour match in gemstones was difficult to achieve because of a lack of suitable examples on the market.

During the 1830s, the design of necklaces remained on the whole unaltered, although the rendering did change and gradually the lacy *cannetille*-work was replaced by *repoussé*-work (*see pp. 104-105*). The common feature of both techniques was their lightness and their sparing use of gold. The *repoussé* technique used mechanical presses to stamp three-dimensional decorative elements. Not surprisingly, both *cannetille-* and *repoussé*-work were characterized by a common decorative repertoire of scallop shells, scrolls and florets, much indebted to the Rococo styles of the 18th century. The range of gems chosen to decorate necklaces of *repoussé* gold was similar to that employed in *canticle* jewels. In some instances the colourful effect was achieved by means of polychrome enamels. Scrolls and floral motifs against black backgrounds in champlevé enamelling were in fact a common alternative to gems at the time.

Since the *parure* or matching set of jewelry was one of the fashion requirements of the day, it is not surprising that a large number of necklaces of the period survive with matching earrings, bracelets, corsage ornaments and even at times hair ornaments. Quite a large number of these necklaces have survived in their original form. Their low gold content and semiprecious gems made them less attractive for breakage and eventual remounting. During the 1820s and 1830s, necklaces set with semiprecious stones or decorated with enamel were most common, but examples mounted with precious gems, especially diamonds, were produced in wealthier countries such as Britain. There, the landed aristocracy was still in a position to commission new necklaces of high intrinsic value, which was certainly not the case in France. It is significant that no diamond-set necklace of the period was illustrated by Henri Vever in *La Bijouterie française*, the authoritative account of the development of French jewelry from the Revolution up to 1908. The designs for necklaces set with highly valuable stones conformed to earlier prototypes and consisted mainly of *rivières* and their variations.

Among surviving *rivières* is an exceptional example set with thirty-seven large diamonds, typically open-mounted in pinched collets. It was given by George IV in around 1820 to his mistress, Lady Conyngham, whose insatiable appetite for jewels was legendary. An especially prominent variation of the *rivière* design was a necklace made of a row of large diamonds encircled by rings of smaller stones.

Mid Nineteenth-century Naturalism

The accession to the throne of the eighteen-year-old Queen Victoria in 1837 marked the beginning of a new era. Her long reign and the values it came to embody are among the most remarkable phenomena of the latter part of the 19th century. The Queen's personal taste both in fashion and jewelry proved so influential that leadership in jewelry design shifted for a time to London rather than Paris.

Even though the decade of the 1840s was a period of extraordinary innovation and upheaval, the subservient position of women in society did not significantly change. Quietness and delicacy were the most admired female qualities, and a woman's aim was to appear always *souffrante* and frail. Pallor was *de rigueur* and often achieved by artificial means, such as drinking vinegar. This was matched in fashion by unprecedented prudery, instigated by Queen Victoria herself. Women covered themselves as never before in long, wide and cumbersome skirts, which concealed feet in flat-heeled slippers. The poke bonnet secured by bows under the chin allowed faces to be seen only from directly in front. Only in evening gowns, characterized by straight-across *décolletés*, was it deemed fitting for women to reveal the pallor of their skin. Day-time fashions left little scope for necklaces, which were largely impeded by collars and ribbons around the neck. But surprisingly, though the *décolletés* of evening wear could have called for necklaces, they do not appear to have been a prominent form of adornment. Extant examples are rare, contemporary portraiture seldom depicts them and, most significantly, they hardly feature in the fashion plates of the day. The reason for this dearth is possibly to be found in the greater emphasis given to large and elaborate bodice ornaments, which consisted of fabric, of gem-set corsage ornaments with *pampille* decorations, or even of bouquets of fresh flowers.

Such necklaces as were made tended to be short and to encircle the base of the neck rather than adorn the *décolleté*, as had been customary in the 1830s. Their designs were largely indebted to the naturalistic motifs in favour at the time: clusters of fruit and berries alternating with leaves. Among the most common were those designed as fruiting vines. Entwined sprays of leaves and flowers such as ivy, orange blossoms, roses and forget-me-nots were also in vogue and were often used to symbolize love and affection. Interest in naturalism, which had been stimulated by artists of the Romantic movement, ran contemporary to the vogue for plant collecting, inspired by the importing and cultivation of new species. Indeed, the leading British writer on aesthetics, John Ruskin, published in the 1850s a series of lectures on the use of natural motifs in the design of

A coloured gold and pearl necklace of grape design with matching earrings, probably English, *c.* 1835–45.

the decorative arts, a source of inspiration which continued throughout the century. But the most typical form of neck ornament of the 1840s and early 1850s was undoubtedly the serpent necklace (*see pp. 110-111*). This usually consisted of the representation of a snake biting its tail, with a heart-shaped pendant suspended from its jaws. The serpent, symbol of wisdom, life and eternity, had wound its way through the history of jewelry design since antiquity. Popular in Greek and Roman jewelry, both for its decorative potential and its talismanic properties, it was revived in the late 1830s in the form of articulated necklaces of gold scale-like linking, the entire body being set with turquoises or diamonds. Less costly versions might consist of a gold body with gem-set heads and tails.

Revivalism and Exoticism, 1860–80

By the mid 1850s, France was once more ruled by an Emperor. The Second Empire opened in an atmosphere of material prosperity and expansionism which intensified during the following decade. In London, Queen Victoria was on the throne as ruler of a wealthy and growing empire. Trade and commerce were flourishing in both countries. This was the age of a triumphant bourgeoisie: bankers, industrialists, merchants and businessmen had come to occupy a more prominent position in society than ever before.

Increasing prosperity meant the increasing elaboration of female dress, and the decades of the 1860s and 1870s saw new heights in eccentricity in fashion. Skirts, supported by enormous crinolines, expanded to impractical dimensions. The Empress Eugénie, the influential wife of Napoleon III, was an enthusiastic exponent of this style of dress and contributed greatly to its popularity. The bust, in contrast, was tightly laced into uncomfortable corsets and the *décolletage* of ball dresses was extremely generous. The collapse of the Second Empire heralded the decline of the crinoline, one of its most potent symbols, and in the 1870s another type of skirt became fashionable. This was bunched out at the back into a bustle and further embellished by a train, even for day wear. The bust continued to be tightly laced and evening wear *décolleté* remained very deep.

Necklaces now came back into great favour and, together with matching earrings, were undoubtedly the most popular form of personal ornament of the time. They were generally short and encircled the base of the neck. The prevailing form consisted of a chain or band supporting a radiating fringe of drops of varying inspiration. This period was characterized by extraordinary artistic eclecticism, coupled with a taste for revivalism, which aimed to enrich the present by looking at the past. This phenomenon, which had been growing during preceding decades, was beginning to influence jewelry designers whose necklaces now embraced archaeological, Egyptian, Gothic and Renaissance revival styles.

The archaeological discoveries at Pompeii and Herculaneum in the 18th century inspired the use of motifs deriving from the Classical world in most decorative arts. It was not until the early 19th century, though, in the wake of Napoleonic Classicism, that these were also applied to jewelry. This interest in ancient jewelry was further stimulated by archaeological excavations from the 1830s onwards. Etruscan jewels were being unearthed from tombs in Cerveteri, Vulci, Chiusi and Orvieto near Rome. Ancient Greek jewels were coming to light at sites in Melos, Rhodes, Knossos and southern Russia. These finds naturally generated considerable interest in the revival of the designs and techniques of ancient jewelry. Both the gold fringe necklaces of the Hellenistic period and the granulation typical of Etruscan work inspired jewelers and served as models for their creations (*see pp. 112-113*).

The centre for archaeological revival jewelry in the Greek and Etruscan styles was undoubtedly Rome, where the Castellani workshop had already become an attraction for foreign visitors by the end of the 1850s (*see pp. 116-117*). The firm produced splendid gold jewelry, using decorative motifs drawn from the Classical repertoire and emulating ancient goldsmiths' techniques, such as granulation. The Castellanis were not alone in

A design for a *grande parure égyptienne* necklace, Lemonnier, Paris, 1869, reproduced by Henri Vever in his *La Bijouterie française au XIXème siècle*, Paris, 1908.

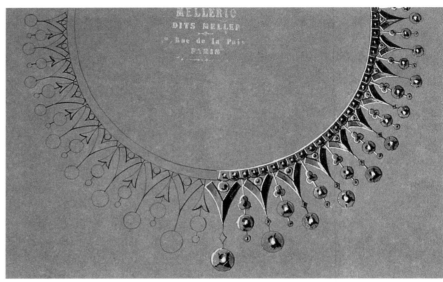

Above left Designs for gold fringe necklaces, Eugène Fontenay, Paris, c. 1870, reproduced in *La Bijouterie française au XIXème siècle*, Paris, 1908.

Above right A design for a diamond-set fringe necklace by Mellerio *dits* Mellers, Paris, late 19th century.

Rome; other jewelers – Ernesto Pierret, Antonio Carli and Antonio Civilotti – were also producing fine ornaments in a Classical revival style. If, at first sight, necklaces in archaeological revival style produced in Rome at this time appear very diverse, they are in fact all characterized by a similar outline of either gold chains or woven bands, from which are suspended radiating fringes of variously shaped pendants, often arranged in multiple tiers. These pendants, closely mirroring their Hellenistic prototypes, were often designed as amphora-shaped drops or elongated seed motifs and decorated with beaded work and granulation. Other examples featured drops decorated with cameos or intaglios depicting mythological scenes. Jewelers working in this style not only copied or reinterpreted examples from the past, but also set genuine fragments from antiquity, such as Roman engraved gems and Greek or Roman coins, in the necklaces. Pomegranates, fruiting vines, leaves and berries, inspired by the Classical world, were also used as pendants. Micromosaic plaques depicting the archaeological ruins of Rome within gold corded wire or beaded work borders were also popular.

In Italy, the second centre for archaeological revival jewelry was Naples, where Giacinto Melillo, notably, who had trained in the Castellani workshop, worked very much in the Roman style (*see pp. 112-113, 122-123*). He produced necklaces immediately derived from Hellenistic prototypes, designed as gold woven bands supporting seed- or leaf-shaped pendants. The techniques of these Italian jewelers were also derived from antiquity. Granulation, mastered by the Etruscans, was extensively used, although it never reached the fineness achieved in the past. Wire-work, beaded-work and enamels, in accordance with ancient practice, were preferred to gemstones as a form of decoration. Likewise, gold – with its solar, warm hue – was the only metal used in the creation of these necklaces, very much harking back to the practices of the Greeks and Etruscans. By the late 1860s, the taste for archaeological revival jewelry had spread throughout

Europe (*see pp. 118-119*). In France the ancient prototypes were interpreted more loosely than by the Italian jewelers. The leading jeweler of the archaeological revival style in Paris was Eugène Fontenay. His necklaces were less derivative from the antique than those of Castellani, and were always permeated by a delicacy and a femininity unknown in the more severe Italian examples (*see pp. 122-123*). Palmettes, rosettes and foliate and floral motifs abound in the design of his neck ornaments. Drops of matt polychrome enamel painted with mythological scenes reminiscent of miniaturized Pompeiian frescoes often adorn his necklaces, in combination with diamonds and gemstones, which were never used in antiquity or in the Italian revival pieces.

In London, Castellani's jewels aroused widespread enthusiasm at the 1862 International Exhibition, influencing the work of jewelers such as John Brogden, Robert Phillips and the Italian-born goldsmith, Carlo Giuliano. Their creations closely mirrored the Italian examples, being mainly of Hellenistic inspiration and designed as woven gold bands fringed with variously designed drops (*see pp. 112-113*). Characteristically, they featured the Hellenistic S-shaped clasp, in common with large numbers of their Italian counterparts.

In Paris, from as early as the 1840s, Renaissance and Gothic styles had inspired famous jewelers such as François Désiré Froment Meurice, but it was not until the 1860s that the style reached its zenith and spread throughout Europe. From then onwards, for

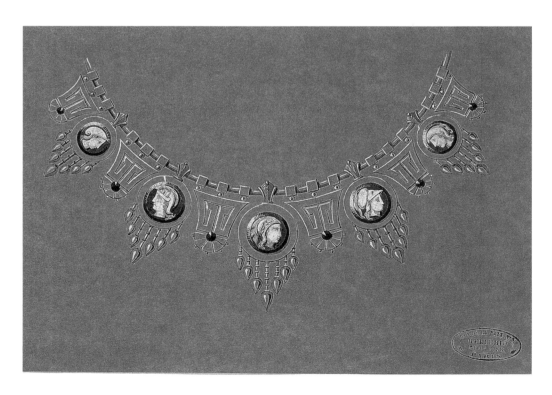

A design for a gold and cameo fringe necklace by Mellerio *dits* Mellers, Paris, *c.* 1875.

A so-called 'Gothic revival' gold, oxidized silver, sapphire and diamond necklace, Austrian, *c.* 1880.

about three decades, jewelry was characterized by sculptural, three-dimensional and figurative shapes. Brightly coloured enamels remained particularly fashionable in France and England where the Romantic Movement had contributed to the revaluation of the Gothic style, seen as an aspect of the cultural heritage of Northern European countries, as opposed to the Classicism of the Mediterranean. Italy, at the time deeply steeped in archaeological revivalism, unsurprisingly, never embraced the style with the same enthusiasm.

Gothic architecture, medieval chivalry, the Italian Cinquecento and the French Renaissance were inexhaustible sources of inspiration for jewelers such as Carlo Giuliano in London, or Froment Meurice, Wièse and Falize in Paris. Their creations were seldom simply replicas of the rare authentic jewels of those periods, but hybrids of both Gothic and Renaissance styles, using elements derived from architecture, sculpture, ceramics, textiles and miniatures. Religious symbolism and heraldry were combined with decorative motifs such as trefoils, crockets, cartouches, leafage and canopied niches. Fantastic creatures such as dragons and griffins, grotesque masks, symbolic figures within architectural frames and elaborate strap- and scroll-work all became favourite subjects in the repertoire of jewelers working in these styles. Polychrome enamel, oxidized silver and coloured gemstones (preferably not faceted but cut *en cabochon* – the typical style of fifteenth- and sixteenth-century jewels) were also favourite materials. Diamonds were used sparingly. Necklaces were short, as required by contemporary fashion.

The rare examples directly inspired by Renaissance prototypes were designed as chains of cartouche and scroll motifs with variously shaped pendants at the front (*see pp. 118-119*). More frequently, though, they were permeated by a general feeling of the Renaissance in their festooned scrolled shapes, in the enamelled decoration and in the emphasis which was placed on settings and decoration rather than on the gemstones. Carlo Giuliano was certainly the most prolific jeweler working in this style loosely inspired by the Renaissance; his production of necklaces designed as chains of foliate scrolls, beautifully decorated with enamels and gemstones, was particularly abundant.

Into this climate of eclectic revivalism finally came the art of Ancient Egypt. As had been the case with the Classical, Gothic and Renaissance revivals, Egyptian art had begun to influence the decorative repertoire of the minor arts earlier in the century, when the Napoleonic campaign in Egypt focused European interest on that mysterious civilization. Jewelers did not become sensitive to this potential source of inspiration until the late 1860s, however, and it was not until the 1867 Universal Exhibition in Paris that jewels in the Egyptian style came into fashion. Another factor was now playing an important role in the promotion of Egyptian art: the publication of Auguste Mariette's papers on his excavations in the Nile Valley, which provided a rich source of new ideas for decorative motifs. Jewelers such as Froment Meurice, Mellerio and Boucheron in France, John Brogden and Robert Philips in England, Castellani and Pierret in Italy were to various degrees sensitive to the influence of pharaonic Egypt. They now produced fringed necklaces with drops in the form of falcons, winged scarabs, lotus flowers and papyri, or similar subjects. Such necklaces were frequently decorated with opaque enamels imitating the white, blue, red and green palette of Egyptian frescoes, together with combinations of gemstones such as rubies, diamonds and turquoises. Faïence and hardstone scarabs, sometimes antique but more often replicas, were also used to fringe gold necklaces. Carlo Giuliano, himself a collector of Egyptian scarabs, was renowned for his bracelets, brooches and stunning necklaces incorporating them or hardstone replicas.

Interest in travel and advances in scientific knowledge, coupled with the mid-century interest in unusual phenomena, significantly affected the jewelry production of the first decades of the second part of the century, influencing design and prompting the introduction of new and exotic materials. Necklaces, in the typical fringed form of the time, were the ideal subject for decoration with drops of unusual shape and for the display of unusual materials. The French campaign in Mexico, for example, is considered to have been instrumental in the introduction of Central and South American themes into fashion; in jewelry, this meant the appearance of gem-set hummingbirds as brooches and hair ornaments. This trend first led jewelers to introduce plumage jewelry into their production; in 1865, Harry Emanuel of London patented his jewels decorated with feathers glued with shellac to a prepared mount. One necklace, bearing his monogram signature, was mounted with seven complete heads and breasts of hummingbirds, their

A portrait photograph of the Duchess of Marlborough, American heiress Consuelo Vanderbilt, wearing a magnificent choker at the coronaton of King Edward VII and Queen Alexandra, 1902 (*see p. 96*).

beaks replaced with gold, applied on shield-shaped trophy supports (*see pp. 114-115*). Equally popular on both sides of the Channel were necklaces set with dried iridescent green Brazilian beetles whose shimmery gleam was often set off by gold mounts in archaeological or Egyptian revival style. The fashion for jewels mounted with birds and beetles of South American origin was an international fad, and it is entirely possible that European firms bought articles already mounted, perhaps in the United States, where the vogue also took hold for necklaces mounted with unusual fauna or with specific parts of a variety of animals. Other unusual organic materials which gained popularity in jewelry at this time included the teeth and the claws of various mammals. Deer teeth became popular in Germany and England about the middle of the century, and necklaces fringed with such novelties were not uncommon, being frequently created as part of entire *parures*. In Britain, close ties with India created a market for jewelry produced in India or in the Indian style in the 1870s, and tiger claws featured prominently in necklaces, set in chased gold mounts and suspended from gold chains (*see pp. 108-109*). Tortoiseshell jewels, inlaid with gold and silver *piqué*-work, had been worn in the first half of the century, but their heyday came in the 1860s, with necklaces designed as strings of the material, variously decorated with gold and silver *piqué*. These remained popular throughout the following decade. Exotic shells, too, attracted the attention of jewelers in their continuous quest for the unusual and the bizarre. Treated like true gemstones, they were carefully encased in gold mountings which did not damage their structure and chained together to form highly decorative necklaces.

The taste for so-called novelty jewelry also developed considerably during these decades. A certain frivolousness invaded jewelry design in the 1860s, the typical fringed necklace of the time being an ideal form of support for pendants in unusual shapes.

Fin-de-siècle

The last decade of the 19th century, a period of profoundly changing values, saw the increasing break-up of traditional social structures, typified by the rise of people who had made new fortunes in business and manufacturing. These included the South African millionaires who were now reaping the riches from the commerce in newly discovered diamonds. The first diamond was found in South Africa in 1867 at a point five hundred miles inland from the Cape of Good Hope, near the source of the Orange River. A passing pedlar noticed some children playing with a handful of stones on the floor of a farmhouse; one of the stones seemed to have its own inner glow and was eventually revealed to be a diamond. It was sold to the Governor of the Cape Colony who exhibited it at the Paris Exhibition of 1867. This incident signalled the beginning of the great diamond rush. Prospectors roamed the African countryside, plunging into rivers and streams and scratching every likely patch of dry earth. By 1875 there were about ten thousand prospectors in Kimberley, some successful, some not. Production became so abundant that prices began to fall alarmingly. In 1888, De Beers Consolidated Mines was formed with the purpose of regulating the output of diamonds to stabilize their price on the market. But diamonds were already relatively abundant and it is not surprising that they became the gemstone *par excellence* of the end of the 19th century, and were mounted to their greatest advantage in the sumptuous necklaces of the period (*see pp. 130-131*).

The high value placed on the decorative qualities of necklaces at this time was largely due to contemporary fashion. From the 1880s until the end of the century the design of lady's skirts had changed from bustles, which fell in intricate swathes of fabric as

Below A fine diamond and pearl tiara forming a necklace, illustrated in the catalogue of the Goldsmiths and Silversmiths Company Ltd., London, 1901.

Foot of page Two pearl and diamond necklaces by Henri Vever, Paris, *c.* 1900, one provided with a tiara fitting.

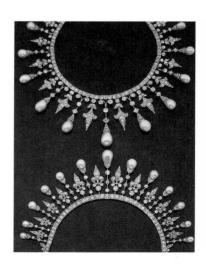

elaborate as curtains, to long bell-shaped skirts, which fell smoothly to the ground. A high bust was obtained by means of a long, stiff, tightly laced corset. This style rendered the chest the focal point of the female silhouette and jewelers concentrated their efforts on adorning this part of the body with necklaces and brooches.

During the day the *décolleté* was concealed by high collars finished with ruching or large bows of tulle. In the evening, however, it was cut low and trimmed with elaborate lace-work or diaphanous fabric. Understandably, necklaces were not part of day-time dress, but with evening gowns they were worn in abundance, as though to compensate for their absence during the day. Three or more necklaces would be worn together, all lavishly encrusted with gems – usually diamonds, which complemented and enhanced the delicate palette of contemporary styles. Subdued hues, such as pearly greys, dusky pinks, lavenders and the softest silvery greens, characterized the dress of an era learning to look at itself and be admired in the new, cold and brash electric light, which also made diamonds sparkle as never before.

The fashionable forms were *rivières*, chokers and fringe necklaces, frequently worn together (*see p. 134*). There were two styles of choker, or *collier de chien*; the simpler form was generally designed as a jeweled central plaque applied either on to fabric or flanked by numerous rows of pearls. The more lavish type was formed of a continuous articulated band entirely set with gemstones. Both were very wide, often consisting of twelve or fifteen rows of seed pearls or as many as the length of the wearer's neck could accommodate. Though elegant, this ornament was clearly not particularly comfortable, as evidenced by its English name of 'choker'. The Duchess of Marlborough, American heiress Consuelo Vanderbilt, could not refrain from complaining about the discomfort she endured while wearing her nineteen-row pearl choker with diamond clasp, acquired during her honeymoon in Paris in 1895. In her autobiography, *The Glitter and the Gold*, she commented, 'Jewels never gave me pleasure and my heavy tiara invariably produced a violent headache, my dog-collar a chafed neck.'

It was essential that chokers should be fitted according to each individual neck. Ready-made examples did not always fit properly and either sagged or choked the wearer. But as always in fashion, discomfort came second to beauty. This elegant ornament remained in favour until 1910, when it was replaced by a more comfortable type of choker, much to the relief of thousands of women. The most common design for such chokers consisted of rows of pearls alternating with diamond-set space bars; stylized foliate motifs and fluttering ribbons, which anticipated the decorative repertoire of the following decades, were used less frequently.

The other form of necklace which was worn at the base of the neck, frequently under the choker, was the 'fringe' necklace (*see pp. 124-125*). Its basic structure was a succession of drop motifs arranged in a fringe-like formation – hence the name – and graduated in size from the centre. Fringe necklaces almost invariably doubled as tiaras. This was made possible by mounting the necklace upside down on a metal hair ornament frame. The drops, a feature of these necklaces, were in a variety of shapes.

(*continued on p. 145*)

BERLIN IRON

This necklace (*above*) dates from *c.* 1810 and is probably German or French; it is formed of oval elements connected by fine chains. Its overall linearity shows Classical influences and the subjects of the medallions are taken from Ancient Greek mythology - typical features in necklaces of the first decades of the 19th century. These were realized in a variety of precious and semiprecious materials. This particular example is made of iron worked into wires and cast into plaques, a technique commonly known as 'Berlin iron'.

The two portraits (*left above* and *below*) show respectively an Italian miniature of the Infanta Maria Isabella of Spain, Queen of Naples, *c.* 1802, and an American painting depicting Harriet Leavens, *c.* 1815; both sitters are wearing early examples of this fashionable necklace type. It consisted of a single central element rather than multiple motifs suspended on fine chains; its popularity throughout Europe and North America was as universal as these examples suggest.

FIRST EMPIRE

These two rare necklaces (*below* and *opposite*), formed respectively of emerald and diamond, and sapphire and diamond clusters, are connected by gem-set chains. Examples like these, particularly fashionable in Napoleonic courtly circles, were the expensive counterparts to popular necklaces of the time formed of gold chains connecting variously decorated plaques (*pp. 97, 100 and 101*). The fine emerald and diamond necklace, part of a suite of jewels probably created by the Parisian jeweler Nitot, founder of the firm of Chaumet, was a wedding gift by Napoleon to his adoptive daughter, Stéphanie de Beauharnais. The portrait by François Gérard (*right*) shows Stéphanie wearing her emerald *parure* in 1806, the year of her marriage to Charles, Prince of Baden. Another portrait by Gérard (*opposite below left*) of 1803 shows the Empress Joséphine wearing a fashionable gem-set necklace, an observation repeated by Louis David in his multiple portrait (*opposite below right*) of the ladies at Napoleon's coronation in 1804.

SENTIMENTAL FESTOONS

Unlike early nineteenth-century necklaces mounted with gemstones of high intrinsic value which were frequently dismantled and their precious stones and metals re-used for more up-to-date ornaments, those set with more humble materials have survived in relatively larger numbers. These necklaces were characteristically designed as multiple-chain festoons connecting cameos, intaglios and mosaic plaques, invariably mounted in very thin sheet gold, making the necklaces very light. This lightness complemented the flimsiness of contemporary dress and at the same time reflected the scarcity of precious metal throughout Europe.

This gold festoon chain necklace (*below*) is decorated wtih eight Florentine hardstone mosaic plaques representing a variety of moths, *c.* 1805. Another necklace of similar date (*opposite above*) is formed of festoons of fine gold chains which connect purple enamel and diamond-set elements. The central motif, inscribed with the word 'Souvenir' in diamonds, suggests this was

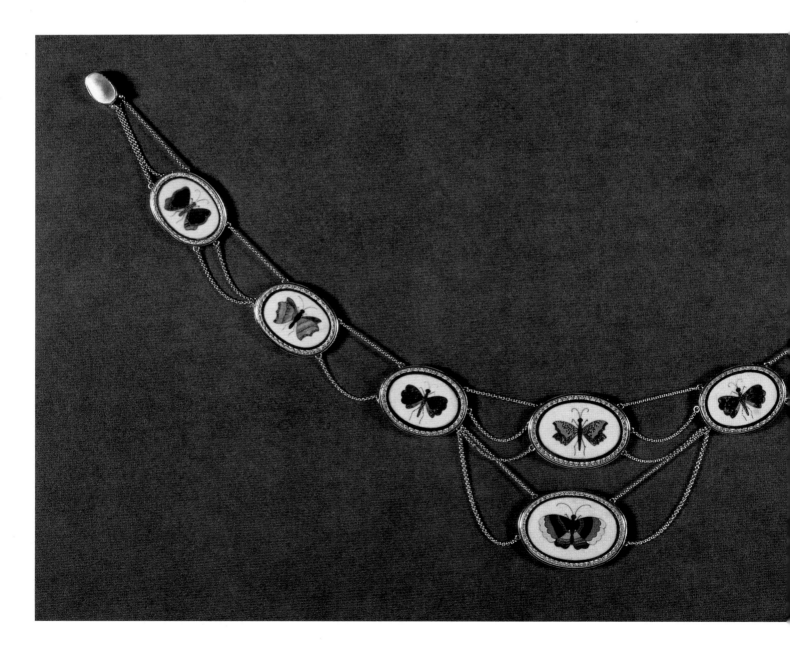

an ornament with sentimental connotations. Both examples illustrate how, by this date, most necklaces were fastened by means of metal spring clasps rather than tied at the back with ribbons threaded through metal loops.

Another two necklace designs (*opposite below*) of similar festooned chain form, dating from the first decade of the 19th century, were recorded by the Parisian jeweler, Eugène Fontenay, in his publication *Les Bijoux anciens et modernes* of 1887.

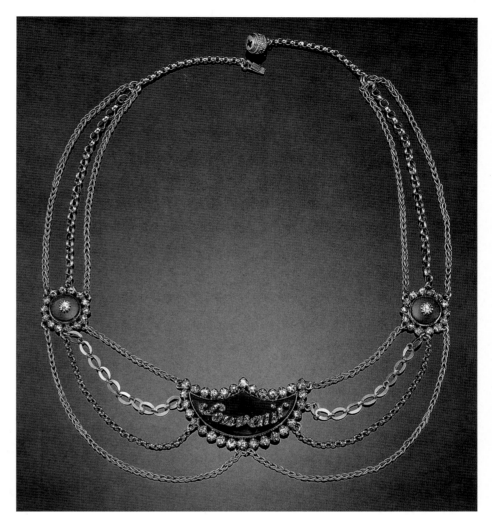

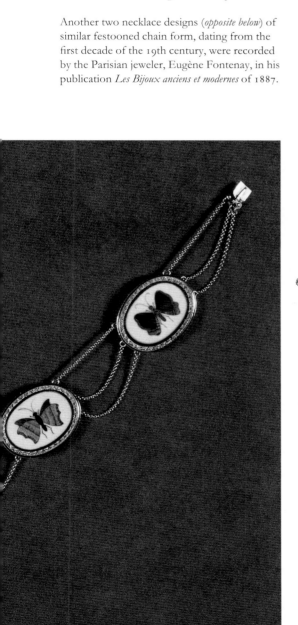

MICROMOSAICS

Necklaces formed of fine gold chains connecting plaques mounted in very plain frames are typical of the early years of the 19th century. The examples shown on these pages are decorated with micromosaics, probably produced in Rome and made of minute polychrome glass tesserae depicting either naturalistic motifs derived from the designs of ancient floor mosaics or architectural views of Rome. The finest examples relied on the use of minute tesserae, subtly shaded and closely fitted. Tourists visiting Rome either purchased them mounted as jewels or bought them individually.

The miniature of a young lady (*below left*) wearing a micromosaic necklace by Louis-Marie Autissier, Brussels, 1829, illustrates the fashionable market for this form of necklace. Simple chains are very much a feature of early nineteenth-century necklaces. These gradually evolved into more elaborate connecting elements as illustrated by the example of *c.* 1820 set with malachite plaques connected by rosette-shaped motifs (*left*).

This Roman necklace (*below*) with a matching pair of earrings is decorated with ten micromosaic plaques connected by fine chains and depicting historic architectural views of Rome, including the Colosseum, the Pantheon and St. Peter's Square. Two gold and micromosaic necklaces (*opposite*) feature floral decorations and birds, the piece *below* inspired by ancient floor mosaics.

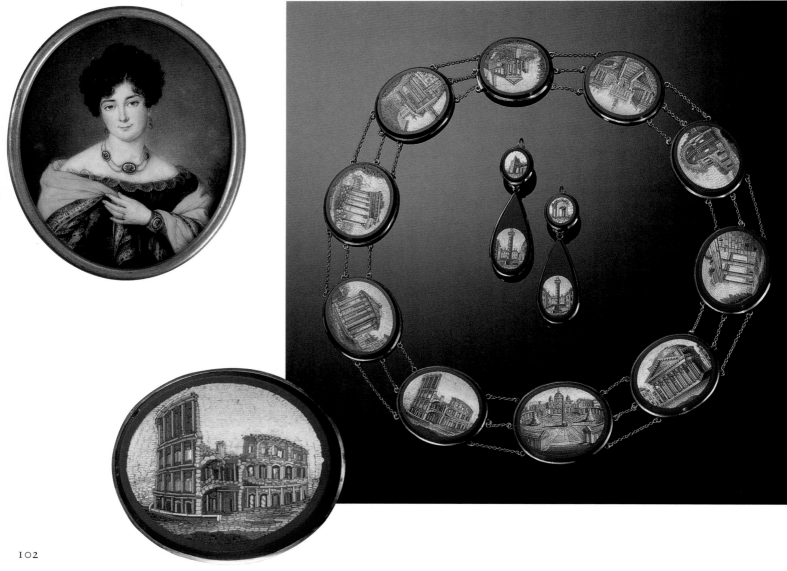

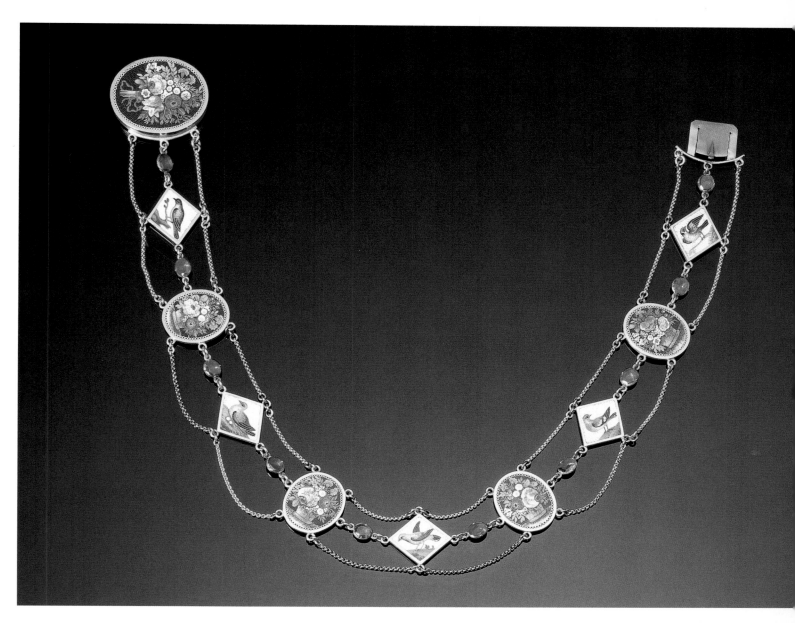

REPOUSSÉ-WORK IN THE 1830s

The necklaces illustrated on these pages are especially representative of their decade. The designs, very much in keeping with contemporary fashion, are reminiscent of eighteenth-century models. Typically, they consisted either of a *rivière* of gems or of gemstone clusters supporting pendants in a variety of interpretations of *girandole*, *pendeloque* and cross motifs.

These examples are (*from top left, anti-clockwise*): a gold *repoussé,* seed pearls and polychrome enamel necklace, probably Swiss, the centre formed of a *girandole* motif; a gold *repoussé* necklace, decorated

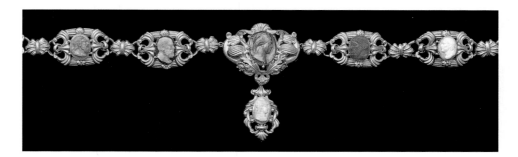

with three shell cameos; a gold *repoussé* necklace formed of scroll-work cartouches set with turquoises; a gold necklace, the centre with a *girandole* motif, decorated with black and white *champlevé* enamel and set with foiled multicoloured gemstones, probably north Italian; a gold *repoussé* necklace decorated with foliate scrolls and shell motifs set with pink topazes; a gold *repoussé* necklace with a *pendeloque* motif at the centre and decorated with hardstone cameos, of which the reverse illustrates the characteristic hollow structure of elements produced with the *repoussé* technique and the possibility of detaching the central element to be worn as a brooch.

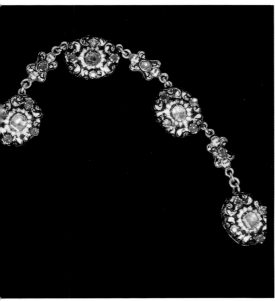

THE LACE-LIKE EFFECTS OF
CANNETILLE

Following contemporary fashion, necklaces made in the *cannetille* technique are reminiscent of eighteenth-century styles. In less lavish examples the gem-set elements were restricted to the front and supported on bands of fine gold mesh. Colour was an essential element of these creations, being provided by gemstones such as pink topazes, greenish-yellow chrysoberyls, purple amethysts and yellow citrines, their hues often intensified by the use of coloured metal foil backings.

The examples on this page are (*from the top*): a pink topaz and gold *cannetille* necklace, the central motif of *girandole* design, on a band of gold mesh; an impressive gold *cannetille* necklace with a cruciform pendant set with emeralds and diamonds (examples set with gems of such high intrinsic value are very rare); a gold *cannetille* necklace with cruciform pendant entirely set with foiled pink topazes and chrysoberyls. Sets of matching jewels were one of the fashion requirements of the day; this particular example of a gold *cannetille* and amethyst *parure* (*opposite*) comprises a necklace with a detachable *girandole* pendant which may be worn also as a brooch, a pair of pendant earrings, and a pair of bracelets.

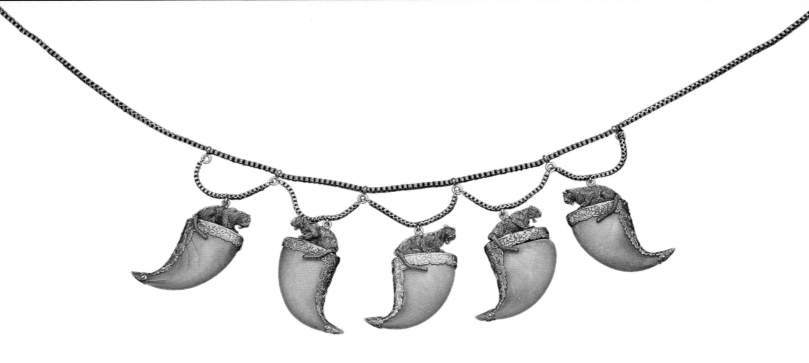

MID-CENTURY EXOTICISM

In Britain, close ties with India created a market for jewelry in Indian style, and tiger claws set in chased gold mounts (*opposite top* and *centre*) featured prominently in necklaces of the 1870s. Exotic shells were also used, and treated as true gemstones; they were carefully encased in gold mountings which did not damage their structure, as in this example (*above* and *left*) produced and cased by John Brogden in London. The taste for novelty jewelry at the time provided a ready market for necklaces with unusual drops, such as the example (*opposite below left*) with three gold butterfly forms.

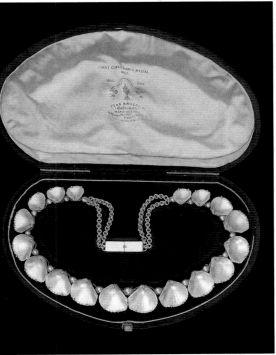

THE SERPENT'S TAIL

The snake, symbol of wisdom, life and eternity had wound its way through the history of jewelry design since antiquity. In the 1840s it became popular in the form of articulated necklaces of scale-like linking often supporting a heart-shaped locket, whereby the symbol of eternity was combined with that of love. Most commonly, serpent necklaces were entirely encrusted with turquoises, while the most precious examples were studded with diamonds. Less expensive examples were of plain gold with head and locket set with gemstones such as carbuncles, emeralds and diamonds.

This gold and turquoise serpent necklace (*above*) incorporates *cabochon* garnet and rose diamond eyes; a similarly decorated example (*left*) has *cabochon* ruby eyes. The two serpent necklaces (*below*), with gold scale-like bodies, have heads decorated respectively with carbuncles, emeralds and diamonds, supporting heart-shaped lockets. *Opposite* is a double-length gold example with cushion-shaped diamonds.

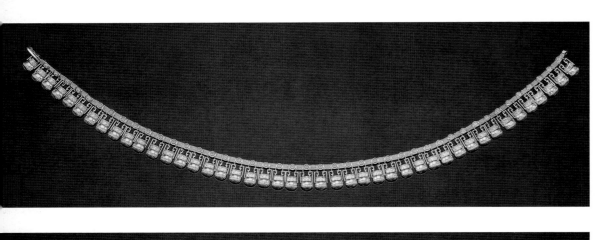

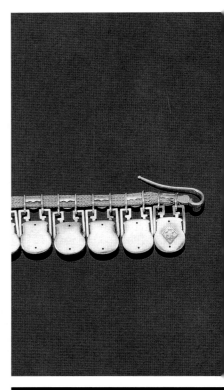

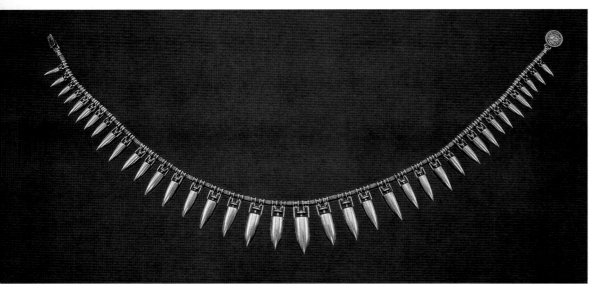

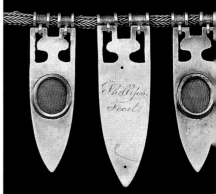

CLASSICAL REVIVALS

Gold fringe necklaces of the Hellenistic period and granulation typical of Etruscan work inspired jewelers for two decades from the 1860s. The centre for this so-called 'archaeological revival' jewelry was Rome, where the workshop of Castellani set the trend. Necklaces in this style were designed as chains or woven bands of gold supporting pendants in the shape of amphorae, drops, shells, seeds, pomegranates, leaves and berries. Most of these necklaces feature eye-and-hook or S-shaped clasps and often bear a mark or a signature of their maker.

This plaster cast of the Princesse Mathilde (*opposite above left*) shows her wearing a fashionable archaeological revival fringed necklace; this likeness was taken from her marble bust executed by Jean-Baptiste Carpeaux in 1862. Cousin of Emperor Napoleon III, she was an influential figure in cultural and artistic circles in Paris throughout the Second Empire. A gold necklace (*opposite above right*) by Carlo Giuliano, *c.* 1870, supports a fringe of shell-shaped drops; it is shown here in its original fitted case.

Two gold fringe necklaces, also made in London, but by Phillips, support amphora-shaped drops (*opposite below*). Note the distinctive mark of Phillips, consisting of two 'Ps' back-to-back together with the Prince of Wales feather, and the reverse of the central amphora-shaped drop signed 'Phillips Fecit' (*details opposite*).

The two gold fringe necklaces (*below top* and *centre*) in archaeological revival style by Giacinto Melillo of Naples, *c.* 1870, are set with, respectively, pomegranate drops and seed drops; they are signed with the monogram 'GM'. Another necklace (*foot of page*) of the same period, by John Brogden of London, has amphora-shaped drops, and is signed 'JB'.

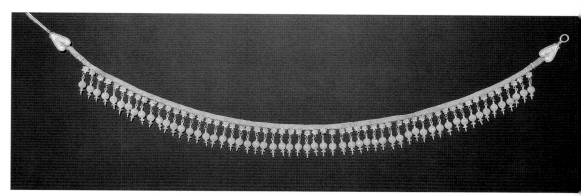

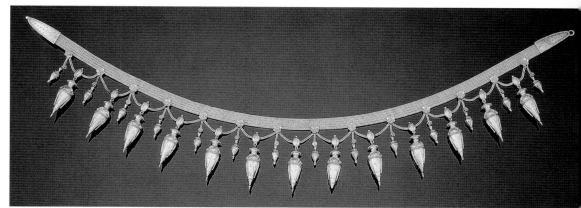

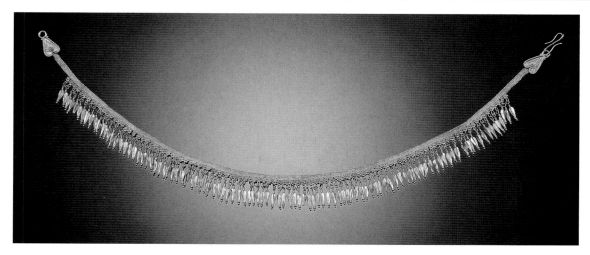

BEETLES AND HUMMINGBIRDS

Necklaces in the fringed form were very popular from the 1860s to the 1880s and were the ideal support for drops of unusual materials. This gold necklace (*opposite above*), loosely archaeological in design, is set with dried iridescent Brazilian beetles, *c.* 1870. Another gold necklace (*opposite below*), of flattened tubular chain, supports a fringe of carbuncles, *c.* 1865. This example is unusual for the emphasis placed on the *cabochon* cut of the gem. The extraordinary gold necklace (*above*) by Harry Emanuel of London, dating from *c.* 1868–70, supports complete heads and breasts of exotic hummingbirds, their natural beaks replaced with gold applied on shield-shaped trophy supports.

THE ARCHAEOLOGICAL ART OF CASTELLANI

The two necklaces illustrated on these pages are superb examples of the archaeological revival style of the last quarter of the 19th century, as interpreted by Castellani of Rome. Both are designed as gold chains supporting vine leaves and bunches of fruiting grapes made of, respectively, cream and purple glass beads. The *finesse* of the craftsmanship and the maker's mark formed of entwined back-to-back 'C's can be seen in the detail (*right*). The unsigned and unmarked example (*opposite*) is shown in its original fitted case stamped with the name of the maker. In common with all Castellani's work, these two examples are obviously derived from Hellenistic jewels, notably earrings from the 3rd–2nd centuries B.C. with designs of fruiting vines, which had been unearthed in southern Italy.

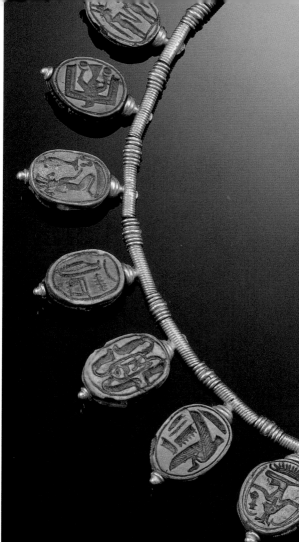

THE TASTE FOR THE PAST

The decades between 1860 and 1880 were characterized by extraordinary artistic eclecticism. The most fashionable necklaces of this period included examples in archaeological, Egyptian, Gothic and Renaissance revival styles. This gold necklace (*opposite*), set by Fontenay with a collection of turquoise cameos depicting mythological scenes and loosely inspired by archaeological prototypes, is softened in its design by the 'feminine' approach typical of the French interpretation of Classical revivalism.

The Carlo and Arthur Giuliano necklace in Egyptian revival style (*above*) is fringed with a collection of glazed steatite pharaonic scarabs. It was fairly common for revivalist jewelers to incorporate genuine fragments from antiquity, such as coins, carved gems or scarabs, in their creations. The Renaissance revival is exemplified in this gold, polychrome enamel, ruby, emerald and diamond necklace and matching bracelet (*right*), c. 1860, unsigned. The chain, designed as a succession of cartouche-shaped motifs, is derived from late Renaissance prototypes.

THE *TIARE RUSSE*

In the last quarter of the 19th century diamonds became pre-eminent among gemstones, largely as a consequence of their relative abundance on the market which followed the opening of the mines in South Africa. They are seen to their greatest advantage mounted in the most sumptuous necklaces of this period, when emphasis came to be placed on size and quality. Among the most fashionable types of necklaces were chokers, *rivières* formed of gemstones or gemstone clusters, and fringe necklaces. The latter were designed as a succession of drop motifs arranged in a fringe-like formation - hence the name - and almost invariably doubled as tiaras. This transformation was executed by mounting the necklace upside down on a metal hair ornament frame. The most impressive type of fringe necklace was that designed as a palisade of lanceolated motifs known as a *tiare russe*.

In this convertible diamond necklace (*below*), *c.* 1880, the clusters can be detached and mounted on tiara, hair-pin, brooch and ring frames. Another impressive diamond necklace is this *rivière* of cushion-shaped diamonds (*foot of page*) supporting at the front a graduated detachable fringe of nine diamond-set drops, *c.* 1880. The inner example of these two variations (*opposite*) of the *tiare russe* was sold in London by D. & J. Welby.

VARIATIONS ON REVIVALISM

By the late 1860s the taste for archaeological revival jewelry had spread throughout Europe, although in France the ancient prototypes were interpreted more loosely than in Italy and in Britain. The gold necklace by Neapolitan jeweler Giacinto Melillo (*above*) and the gold and enamel necklace (*opposite*) by Eugène Fontenay perfectly illustrate this difference. The gold fringed necklace by Melillo is almost an exact reproduction of a stunning Etruscan example from Ruvo, dating from the early 5th century B.C. (*pp. 14–15*). The gold necklace by Fontenay, on the other hand, is permeated by a delicacy and femininity uncommon in the more severe Italian production.

THE GOLD FRINGE

Necklaces designed as a succession of drop motifs arranged in fringe-like formation and graduated in size from the centre were at the height of their popularity in the 1860s and 1870s. These pages illustrate the variety of designs whose inspiration in all instances is indebted to ancient Hellenistic prototypes; these nineteenth-century creations were made of gold purposely matted to imitate the patina of their Classical forebears. They were frequently worn with matching pendant earrings, as we can see in this portrait photograph of Princess Alice, second daughter of Queen Victoria (*left*) wearing a necklace of amphora-shaped drops with earrings *en suite*. These two variations (*below*) on gold fringes, are probably English.

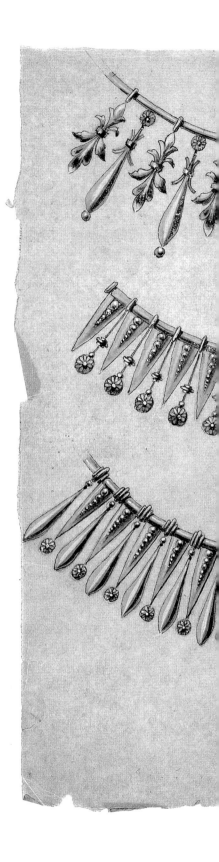

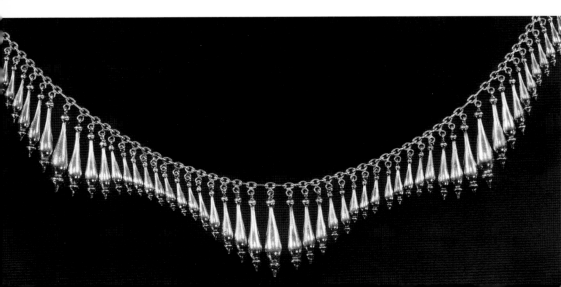

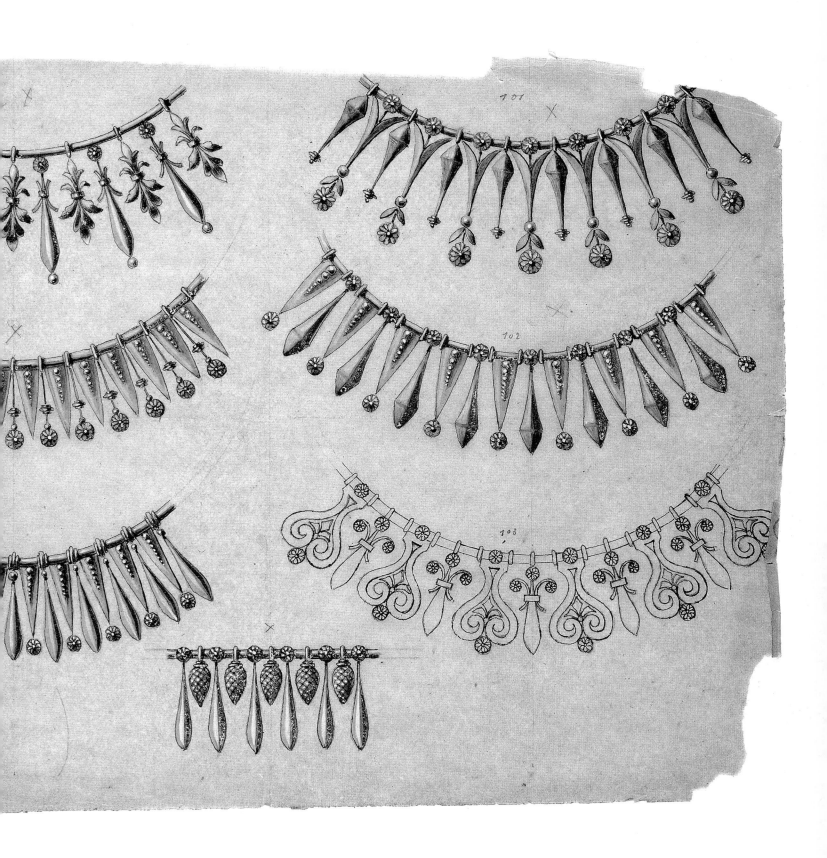

Seven designs for gold fringe necklaces by the renowned Parisian firm, Mellerio, 1870s.

ART NOUVEAU — The brilliant design by Georges Fouquet (*opposite*), *c.* 1904–5, is decorated with *plique-à-jour* enamel-work and set with opals, aquamarines, hessonite garnets and diamonds. The sinuous lines are inspired by nature - in this instance, seaweed - and the emphasis is on form rather than the intrinsic value of precious materials. In this choker (*below*) by René Lalique, *c.* 1900, the central *plaque de cou* bears a chrysanthemum design; the centres of the flowers are carved in opal with petals enamelled in shades of yellow and mauve; the diamond-set border is supported by fifteen rows of seed pearls. The portrait by Gustav Klimt (*detail, above*) of Fritza Riedler, 1906, depicts the sitter wearing a similarly designed choker formed of fifteen rows of pearls and a central decorative element.

IN THE NOUVEAU STYLE

Although pure Art Nouveau jewelry design was relatively short-lived, lasting only from about 1890 to 1905, it stimulated the creation of a number of quite extraordinary neck ornaments by more conventional jewelers, using decorative materials not necessarily of high value, such as glass paste and enamels, in sinuous forms obviously inspired by nature.

These two necklaces (*right* and *below*), set with diamonds by Masriera of Barcelona, are decorated with *plique-à-jour* enamels in shades of green and russet. The silver-gilt, *plique-à-jour* enamel and baroque pearl necklace (*opposite above left*) was sold by the Parisian jeweler, Beaudouin.

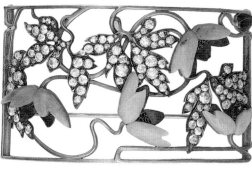

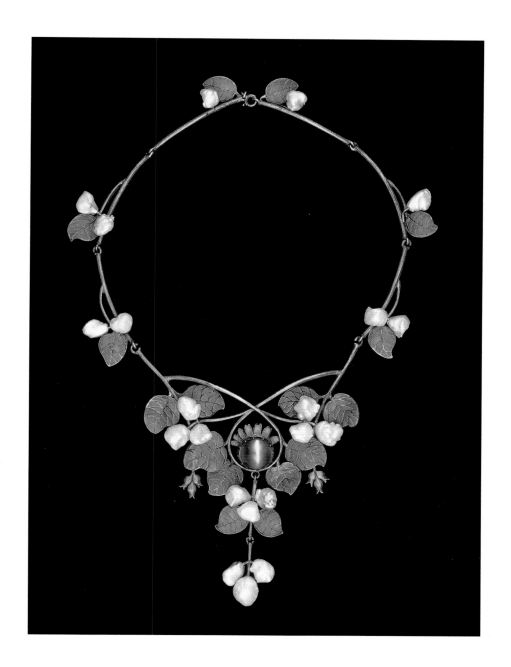

The choker with eighteen rows of seed pearls (*below*) has a *plaque de cou* decorated in shades of orange and green *guilloché* enamel. The examples of gold *plaques de cou* (*above*) are by Vever (attributed) (decorated with moss-green *plique-à-jour* enamel embellished with seed and baroque pearls), and by Lalique (set with opals and diamonds with enamel decoration).

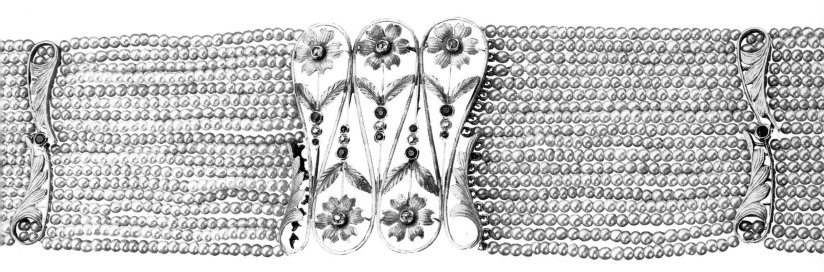

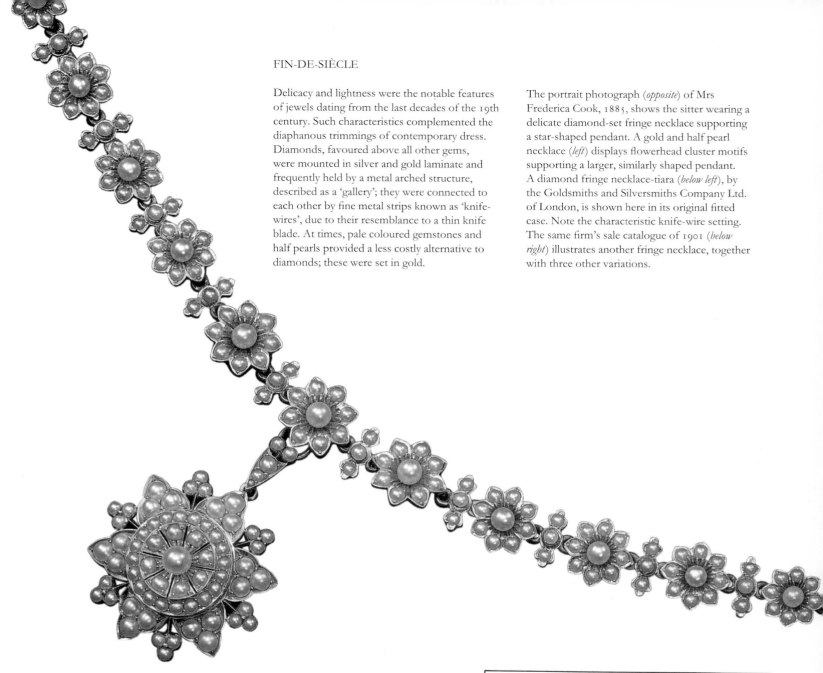

FIN-DE-SIÈCLE

Delicacy and lightness were the notable features of jewels dating from the last decades of the 19th century. Such characteristics complemented the diaphanous trimmings of contemporary dress. Diamonds, favoured above all other gems, were mounted in silver and gold laminate and frequently held by a metal arched structure, described as a 'gallery'; they were connected to each other by fine metal strips known as 'knife-wires', due to their resemblance to a thin knife blade. At times, pale coloured gemstones and half pearls provided a less costly alternative to diamonds; these were set in gold.

The portrait photograph (*opposite*) of Mrs Frederica Cook, 1885, shows the sitter wearing a delicate diamond-set fringe necklace supporting a star-shaped pendant. A gold and half pearl necklace (*left*) displays flowerhead cluster motifs supporting a larger, similarly shaped pendant. A diamond fringe necklace-tiara (*below left*), by the Goldsmiths and Silversmiths Company Ltd. of London, is shown here in its original fitted case. Note the characteristic knife-wire setting. The same firm's sale catalogue of 1901 (*below right*) illustrates another fringe necklace, together with three other variations.

131

QUESTION MARKS

These two spectacular 'question mark' spring *lierre* (*left*) and *coquelicot* (*right*) necklaces set entirely with diamonds mounted in silver and gold laminate were designed by Paul Legrand for Boucheron, Paris, in 1882 and 1883 respectively. From the early 1880s some jewelers working in the mainstream of traditional jewelry began to impart to their creations an unexpected lightness and sinuous line suggestive of the style of the high Art Nouveau designers.

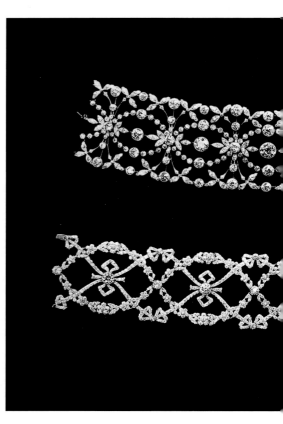

THE ADVENT OF THE CHOKER

Wide chokers set either with diamonds or pearls were at the height of their popularity from 1885 to 1910. Those created after 1900 may be distinguished from earlier examples by their decoration of entwined garland motifs, fluttering ribbons and trophies of love derived from eighteenth-century motifs. Characteristically, they were mounted in platinum rather than silver and gold and frequently backed by bands of fabric in a way reminiscent of the previous century.

The portrait of the Princesse de Broglie (*left*) by James Tissot, *c.* 1895, whose work is remarkable for the brilliance of its record of contemporary Parisian high life, shows the elegant and fashionable sitter wearing a choker set with diamonds backed by cobalt blue fabric. An archive photograph (*above*) of five chokers by Boucheron, 1903–1905, shows examples with diamonds and backed with black velvet.

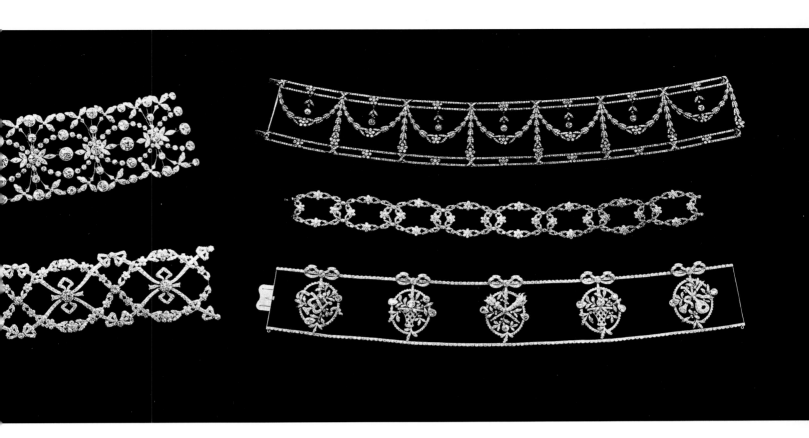

White gouache designs for diamond-set fringe necklaces (*below*) by Mellerio *dits* Mellers, Paris, *c.* 1890; these examples illustrate the contemporary popularity of the diamond-set fringe necklace, which had already begun to show a greater delicacy and lightness compared to that of the previous decades.

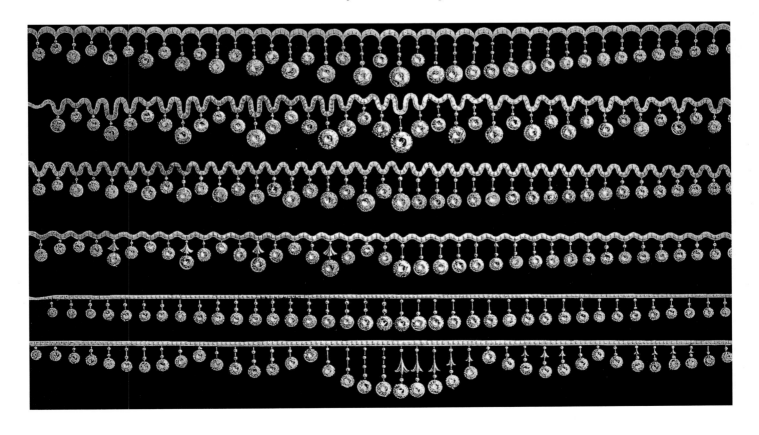

BELLE ÉPOQUE

Lace-like scalloped-shaped necklaces, often worn in conjunction with wide chokers, were the height of fashion in personal adornment during the early years of the 20th century. Their decoration included swags, garlands of leaves, flowers, trellis-work and ribbon bows reminiscent of the Louis Seize style. They were mainly encrusted with diamonds mounted in platinum which had replaced the nineteenth-century laminate of gold and silver. This precious white metal had not been used before on a large scale, mainly because of the difficulty of working it: it has a melting point much higher than that of any other metal then used in jewelry. Its great advantage is that, unlike silver, it is

untarnishable and of great strength. Its use enabled for the first time the creation of jewels which were at once structurally very sound yet delicate and lacy in appearance.

These two scallop necklaces (*above* and *opposite above*) are mounted entirely with diamonds; note especially in the example *opposite* the fine fret-work in platinum which conveys a lace-like quality to the piece. Two other examples (*opposite below*) are set with diamonds highlighted with rubies; the necklace on the *right* was sold by Garrard & Co. of London. Typically, the diamonds are mounted in white metal, while the rubies are in gold.

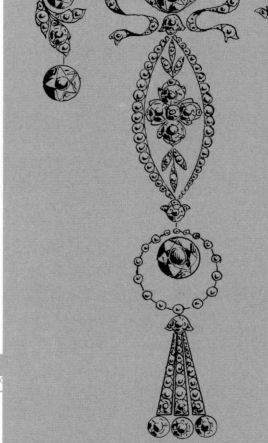

THE GARLAND STYLE

The illustrations in ink on these pages are taken from the design books of August Frederik Hollming, St. Petersburg workmaster for Carl Fabergé; they are dated respectively from *left* to *right*, 1909, 1910, 1911, 1912. All these designs feature mainly diamonds and rely on the use of floral festoon and garland motifs to create a lace-like quality which complemented contemporary dress. Both the Russian Fabergé and the French jeweler Cartier were leaders in this style of early twentieth-century jewelry, often described as 'garland style' due to the almost ubiquitous presence of foliate and floral garland motifs derived from the Louis Seize style.

Июль 31   Колье-брошь   сер-плат:

1 брил.   4 27/.
5   "   10 16/.
20   "   15 5/.
31   "   10 25/.   } сиб.
157   "   10 29/.
60 роз.

добав.: 21 розан N 5
9 " " 6
97 " " 6
312 " " 7
287 " " 8
97 " " 9

THE *SAUTOIR*

Around 1910 a new style of dress began to appear, largely inspired by the creations of French couturier Paul Poiret. This abandoned the corset in favour of tunic forms in soft drapery. In jewelry, at the same time, the choker began to give way to the elongated necklace known as the *sautoir*, which perfectly complemented the new column-like silhouette. These new forms (approximately 75 cm long, excluding pendants) were made up mainly of bands or ropes of woven seed pearls supporting pendants of geometrical shape or tassels. Such exotic trimmings may have been inspired by the vogue for Orientalism in design inspired by Diaghilev's Russian Ballet. The favoured gemstones continued to be pearls and diamonds mounted in platinum with *millegrain* setting, but the earlier fluttering ribbon bows and garland motifs were replaced by more pronounced geometrical elements which already anticipate the style of 1920s.

The group of four platinum, pearl and diamond *sautoirs* (*opposite below left*), *c.* 1910–15, is characterized by designs which are more geometrical, while the garland motifs, when used, are more restrained. It is interesting to note that the pendant in the second example from *left* conceals a watch. Another *sautoir* (*opposite above left*), set with platinum, diamonds and pearls, *c.* 1910, has black silk *gros* instead of seed pearl bands. This fine *sautoir* (*left*) formed of seed pearls, supporting a detachable double tassel motif embellished with calibrated sapphires by Cartier, Paris, *c.* 1924, indicates its slightly later date by the absence of garland motifs. Another Cartier creation, of slightly earlier date, is this platinum and pearl mesh chain *sautoir* (*below*), supporting a detachable pearl and diamond tassel pendant.

AN ALL–PURPOSE *SAUTOIR*

This fine platinum and diamond *sautoir* dates from *c.* 1915; its transitional features make it
a particularly interesting jewel. The decorative repertoire of foliate garland motifs looks to
early twentieth-century styles, while its chunky and more massive proportions foreshadow
those of the 1920s. Characteristically, as is the case for most *sautoirs* entirely set with
diamonds, this necklace can be broken up to create other forms: it may be shortened; it
divides to form two bracelets; and both pendants can be detached and worn separately.

DIAMONDS FOR A DIVA

The famous American opera singer, Lillian Nordica (*above*), photographed here *c.* 1905, stated frequently that the sight of her diamonds never failed to lift her spirits. This image provides a vivid illustration of the extraordinary popularity with society ladies at this time of pearl and diamond necklaces as well as other ornaments. Typically, Miss Nordica's fashionable deep *décolleté* is adorned both by a lavish diamond *résille* necklace and by long strands of fine natural pearls draped around the neck and over the shoulders. She is also portrayed wearing her famous 1905 Cartier tiara mounted with 21 diamond *briolette* drops and her stomacher set with a collection of rare coloured pearls.

The diamond *dentelle* choker (*right*) was made by Boucheron, Paris, 1904; the central bow motifs can be detached and worn separately as a brooch. The lace–like patterning of the gemstones and metals is undoubtedly a reflection of the contemporary passion for lace applied to every part of evening gowns. Jewelers were here rivalling couturiers in luxury trimming.

These included single-stone pendants, circular clusters, trefoils and dart-shaped motifs. Among the most impressive type of fringe necklace was that designed as a graduated palisade of lanceolated motifs, known as a *tiare russe* when worn as a hair ornament (*see pp. 120-121*). Introduced during the 1840s, it became especially fashionable in the latter part of the 19th century. Its shape was allegedly inspired by that of the *kokoshnik*, a form of gabled headdress traditionally worn by Russian women in rural areas – a far cry from the tiara.

The ever-present *rivière* necklace was also at the height of its popularity in this period; it was often worn in combination with either one or both of the necklace forms described above. When made of a succession of diamond clusters, these *rivières* were very versatile and frequently divided into various elements which could be transformed by means of appropriate fittings into pendants, brooches, hair ornaments, rings and earrings. The abundance of diamonds on the market allowed jewelers to create examples set with gems which were perfectly matched in shape, colour and clarity, and perfectly graduated. Often, the individual diamonds which formed such *rivières* were of remarkable size. Fresh emphasis came to be placed on quality – a direct consequence of the large output of new diamonds from South Africa. Cutters were able to avail themselves of a wide choice of rough material and could afford a high waste percentage in the cutting process. Rather than achieve a given weight, the principal aim was to cut the best possible faceted gem. This was helped by the mechanization of the cutting process and a greater understanding of how to manipulate the proportions of faceted diamonds to maximize their light-reflective properties.

The characteristic feature of all late nineteenth-century *rivières* is that the stones were mounted in open-backed collets. These are held by claws supported by a metal arched structure, commonly described as a 'gallery', which allows light to penetrate the pavilion, the lower part of the stone. This type of setting, which was not limited to *rivières*, benefited diamonds in particular. All necklaces set with diamonds continued to be mounted with a silver and gold laminate, which had become the standard method during the century. The silver surrounded the diamond to enhance its whiteness, while gold lined the back of the jewel in order to prevent staining from the silver tarnish. Another distinguishing feature of jewels of this time, especially of necklaces, is the frequent use of the so-called 'knife wire'. This consisted of a fine metal strip, as thin as a knife blade, which was used to connect the various elements of a necklace, giving the impression that they were suspended in mid air. Indeed, delicacy and lightness were common features of the jewels of this time, characteristics which complemented the diaphanous trimmings of contemporary dress (*see pp. 132-133*). Innovations in setting – open-work galleries and unobtrusive knife wire – were also the result of an increased interest in the quality of the gemstone itself. The former emphasis on elaborate and complex mounts was now replaced by an emphasis on gems, which could be admired in all their beauty thanks to simple, functional and unobtrusive settings (*see p. 135*).

A page from the catalogue of Mappin and Webb Ltd., London, 1900, illustrating fine gold and pearl necklaces.

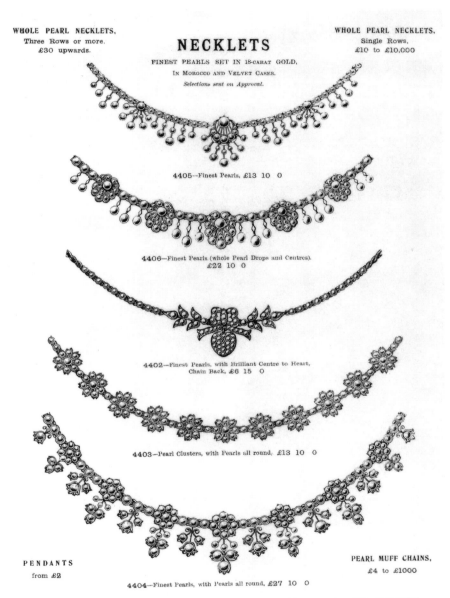

WHOLE PEARL NECKLETS,
Three Rows or more.
£30 upwards.

WHOLE PEARL NECKLETS,
Single Rows,
£10 to £10,000.

NECKLETS

FINEST PEARLS SET IN 18-CARAT GOLD,
IN MOROCCO AND VELVET CASES.
Selections sent on Approval.

4405—Finest Pearls, £13 10 0

4406—Finest Pearls (whole Pearl Drops and Centres).
£22 10 0

4402—Finest Pearls, with Brilliant Centre to Heart,
Chain Back, £6 15 0

4403—Pearl Clusters, with Pearls all round, £13 10 0

PENDANTS
from £2

PEARL MUFF CHAINS,
£4 to £1000

4404—Finest Pearls, with Pearls all round, £27 10 0

Owing to the rise in price of Pearls, prices quoted for Necklets as above in previous lists are cancelled

Together with diamonds, pearls were also favoured for these lavish creations; their sheen complemented both the brilliance of the diamonds and the delicate hues of contemporary dress. They were very highly prized and all shapes and sizes, ranging from the smallest seed pearl to the largest specimens, were employed in conjunction with diamonds. Nor was it uncommon to wear several rows of pearls variously draped on the *décolleté* beneath the choker and the fringe necklace. Necklaces of lesser intrinsic value followed the same designs as those for diamonds and pearls, occasionally scaled down in size. They were mounted with coloured gemstones such as peridots, amethysts, pink topazes and aquamarines. Pale opals and half pearls were also in vogue, the latter mounted in gold and designed mainly as festoons of floral and foliate motifs.

Art Nouveau

Parallel to the developments of mainstream jewelry, the end of the 19th century saw the birth of a new trend in jewelry design related to the international style generally known as Art Nouveau (*see pp. 126-127*). Many of the jewelers who embraced these new aesthetics did so because they were appalled by the poor quality of much mass-produced jewelry, a result of technical progress and increasing mechanization. Much late nineteenth-century jewelry production consisted of ornaments in very low-carat gold in repetitive designs, roughly made and badly finished, and widely available at low prices. At the same time, in high jewelry, excessive exploitation of revivalist motifs and research into past decorative styles had tended to hold back innovation in jewelry design. Furthermore, the greater availability of diamonds had contributed to a shift in emphasis from design to the gems themselves. As a consequence, intrinsic value came to overshadow artistic merit.

Art Nouveau jewelers, in their quest to improve and elevate contemporary design, set out to create jewels inspired by nature, in which materials were subordinate to the design and creativity was more important than intrinsic value. Their aim was to evoke, to interpret nature rather than to copy it. Although, in a sense, the decorative motifs were similar to those of the nineteenth-century naturalistic tradition, they were a departure from imitative realism. Insects and animals were transformed into fantasy creatures; flies and bumble bees gave way to dragonflies and damselflies. Eglantines and roses were supplanted by a more unusual and exotic flora of orchids and wilting chrysanthemums. This iconography was generally set off by the ubiquitous use of curving and sinuous lines.

Like their more conventional contemporaries, however, Art Nouveau jewelers created neck ornaments which conformed to the two main *fin-de-siècle* types: the choker, most frequently formed of a central plaque strung on pearls, and the short necklace which encircled the base of the neck. But if the form of the necklace conformed to mainstream high jewelry fashion, this was certainly not the case in terms of choice of material. Art Nouveau necklaces did not rely on large quantities of diamonds and conventionally precious gems such as rubies and sapphires. Materials were always selected for the part they could play in the overall design and not for their intrinsic value. Horn, pale opal, moonstones, chrysoprase, agate, pearl and moulded *pâte de verre* were preferred to diamonds and coloured precious stones. Enamel was also greatly favoured by Art Nouveau jewelers. They made use of a variety of techniques, the most characteristic of which was the so-called *plique-à-jour*, an open-backed enamel, whose effect resembles that of a stained glass window. Characteristically, the palette both of the gems and of the polychrome enamels consisted of pale and subdued colours.

Although the Art Nouveau style was relatively short-lived in jewelry, lasting only from the end of 1880s to about 1905, it stimulated the creation of a number of quite extraordinary neck ornaments (*see pp. 128-129*). French designer René Lalique, a true innovator, may be regarded as the genius of Art Nouveau jewelry. His work, especially after the Paris Exposition Universelle of 1900, became a model for jewelers both in Europe and America. Parisian jewelers Fouquet, Gaillard, Gautrait and Vever, Barcelona-based Masriera, and Marcus and Tiffany of New York, are only a few of the many jewelry firms who produced work distinctly influenced by Lalique.

Although the design innovations of Art Nouveau were embraced by only a relatively small number of jewelers who were particularly concerned with design problems and who were patronized by a small avant-garde clientèle, they had a much wider influence. Jewelers working in the mainstream of traditional jewelry began in some instances to impart to their creations an unexpected lightness, movement and fluidity, a clear debt to Art Nouveau. The Parisian firm Boucheron, for example, from the late 1880s created a number of stunning neck ornaments. Known as 'question mark' necklaces, these were conceived as diamond-encrusted representations of branches of ivy, cascades of leaves and seeds, or sprays of poppies, all twisted into sinuous and sensual forms which encircled the neck and fell under the chin (*see pp. 132-133*). The fact that these necklaces were lavishly set with diamonds and that their design was in line with the nineteenth-century tradition of naturalistic realism firmly places them in the category of high jewelry. But their sinuous forms are clearly indebted to the curving lines of Art Nouveau design and may be considered a successful compromise between tradition and innovation.

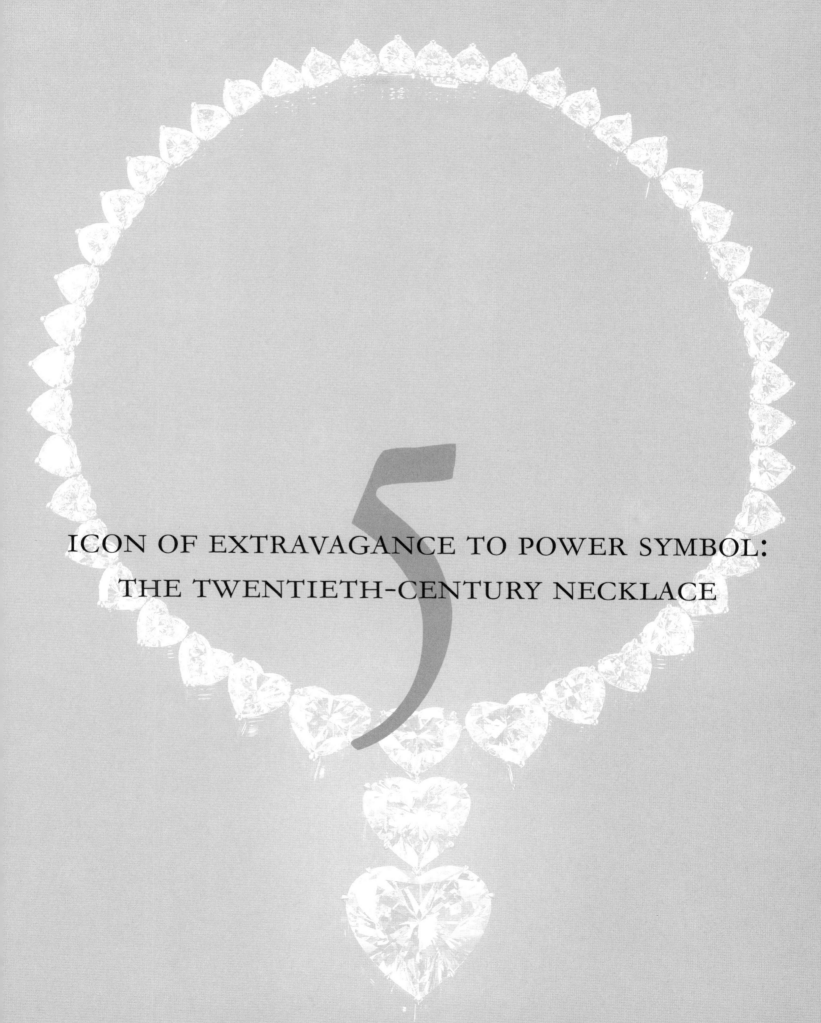

ICON OF EXTRAVAGANCE TO POWER SYMBOL:
THE TWENTIETH-CENTURY NECKLACE

*T*he period from the beginning of the century to the outbreak of World War I was an age of great ostentation and massively increased prosperity, both in Europe and North America, where industrialists and entrepreneurs amassed vast fortunes. In 1901, for instance, the United States Steel Company had been sold to J.P. Morgan for a billion dollars, and more than one thousand Americans accumulated fortunes in excess of one million dollars. These new millionaires and their wives flocked to the Old World, intent on emulating and possibly out-doing the style of the old European aristocracy. Paris was their principal destination and there they bought all the latest fashionable luxury accessories.

Fashion and the Necklace in the Belle Époque

The dress of the first decade of the 20th century relied heavily on the deployment of lavish materials: cascades of lace applied to every part of the gown, complemented by plumes and ostrich-feather boas. The use of the 'health corset', which made the body rigidly straight in front by throwing forward the bust and pushing back the hips,

Left A portrait photograph of Mrs George J. Gould, New York, 1907, wearing her choker and pearl necklaces.

Right A lady portrayed in a Doucet dinner dress in *Les Modes*, 1909; note the combination of short and long pearl necklaces.

produced the characteristic S-shaped posture of the period, further enhanced by full-length, bell-shaped skirts. This fashion made the neck and chest the focal points of the dress; in day-time wear, these were concealed by lace, tulle and straight collars tightly fitted to the neck by means of boning; in the evening they were revealed by extravagantly low-cut *décolletés,* suitably adorned by necklaces whose design resembled that of lace-work (*see pp. 136-137*).

In a period in which dress fashion emphasized the *décolleté,* it was no coincidence that necklaces were favoured above all other jewels. The fashionable shape was the choker, a form of necklace which had already appeared in France in the 1860s and in England around 1880 (*see pp. 162-163*). These chokers were conceived as wide bands, closely hugging the neck; realized in a variety of materials, they were sometimes referred to as *colliers de chien,* due to their resemblance to dog collars. In that age of ostentatious display they were not worn alone, as might be the case nowadays, but rather combined with a number of other necklaces worn at the base of the neck and cascading down the corsage.

Four types of early twentieth-century chokers may be distinguished, varying between 4 and 6 cm in height. The first consists of a shaped gem-set plaque fitted either to strands of pearls, a black velvet band or a silk ribbon; the second, a band of black velvet or silk applied with a continuous gem-encrusted lace-like pattern; the third, a band entirely strung with pearls or set with gemstones; and the fourth, the most lavish, sometimes referred to as *résille* or *draperie de décolleté,* similar to the third, but with decoration extending down the *décolleté* (*see p. 161*).

The prevailing passion for lace in every part of the gown was transposed to the choker in the lace-like patterning of the gemstones and metals (*see p. 144*). While couturiers concealed the neck and bodice of the fashionable lady with costly lace during the day, jewelers strove to conceal the neck and *décolleté* of their discerning clients with lace-like jewels for the evening. The designs of such chokers were of entwined foliate garlands and festoons, ribbon bows and trophies of music and love (*see pp. 138-139*). These motifs were taken up from the latter half of the 18th century and owe a considerable debt to the decorations found in Louis Seize applied arts, such as ormolu furniture fittings, snuff boxes and stucco architectural details. This particular revival was probably indebted for its success to the splendour, pomp and grandeur of eighteenth-century Versailles, which somehow corresponded to the aspirations and illusions of the Edwardian patrons – industrialists, entrepreneurs and financial speculators. Among the most striking examples of the early twentieth-century choker were those realized by Cartier and Fabergé, leaders in the style, and those created by other eminent Parisian jewelers, such as Boucheron, Chaumet and Mellerio.

The three staple ingredients of garland-style chokers were diamonds, pearls and platinum; the latter material began to be used extensively for diamond-set jewelry around the turn of the century, replacing the nineteenth-century laminate of gold and

Opposite Two designs for pearl and diamond chokers by August Frederik Hollming, St. Petersburg workmaster for Carl Fabergé, 1909.

Below Engraved designs for comb mounts and a *chatelaine* from Pouget's *Traité des pierres precieuses*, Paris, 1762.

A diamond *lavallière*, with rings, *c.* 1905.

silver. This precious white metal had not been used before on a large scale, mainly because of the difficulty of working it, due to its having a melting point much higher than that of any other metal then used in jewelry. The great advantage of platinum is that, unlike silver, it is an untarnishable white metal of great strength. Its use enabled for the first time the creation of jewels which were at once structurally very sound, yet delicate and lacy in appearance. This effect was further enhanced by the characteristic *millegrain* setting, the beading of the platinum surrounding the stones which made the metal appear frothy and more lace-like. Given the fashionable interest in the 18th century, it is not surprising to discover that this technique was inspired by the stone mounting of the end of that century.

Pearls and diamonds were the favourite gems and were often combined together. Their appeal, above that of all other gems, lay in their whiteness, sheen and reflective qualities, particularly suited for the rendering of lace-like ornaments and providing an ideal complement to the pale palette of fashionable dress. It was certainly no accident that pearls and diamonds were especially favoured: they were among the costliest gems of the day. Some indication of the high value of pearls at this time is given by the famous transaction between Pierre Cartier and banker Morton F. Plant in 1917. A two-row pearl necklace valued at one million dollars was exchanged by Cartier for a six-storey Renaissance-style mansion on Fifth Avenue, which then became the headquarters of Cartier in New York. And the ostentation with which diamonds were flaunted at social gatherings, such as opera and theatre performances, was quite extraordinary. The thirty-five boxes of the Metropolitan Opera House in New York became such a dazzling showcase that they were referred to as 'The Diamond Horseshoe'.

The choker, as we saw above, was not worn alone but in conjunction with other forms of necklaces which hung at the base of the neck. These included *rivières*, strings of pearls, *lavallières* and scalloped collars. The *rivières* were set with large diamonds, while the strings of pearls were made up of fine natural specimens; both were worn long and in large numbers. They cascaded down the front of the dress and, as we can see from a 1907 portrait photograph of Margherita, Dowager Queen of Italy, were occasionally so long that they reached the knees.

The *lavallière*, in vogue from 1900, consisted of a stylized knotted motif supporting pendants of uneven lengths. Its name was derived from that of the French actress Eve Lavallière, whose former occupation had been that of tying ribbons in a hat factory. The cravats which were produced in this way were called *lavallières* and thus provided a stage name for the actress born Eve Ferroglio. Once again, they were usually set with pearls and diamonds. The scalloped collars, reminiscent of lace-work, were rendered in platinum and diamonds, occasionally enhanced by coloured gemstones (*see pp. 136-137*). Their decorative repertoire is similar to that of chokers, and includes swags, garlands of leaves and flowers, trellis-work and ribbon bows.

A dramatic new influence on dress fashion and style made itself felt around 1910 and almost immediately prompted a change in the shape of necklaces. There has been much speculation as to whether this change was brought about first by Diaghilev's Russian Ballet or by the Parisian couturier Paul Poiret; whatever the timing, the conjunction of the two was devastating. A wave of Orientalism in design and fashion was prompted by the performance in 1910 of *Schéhérazade* in Paris: the costumes, inspired by Oriental harems, were in colours which seemed amazingly garish compared with those of classical ballet. In dress, the pale pastels of the early years of the century were swept away and the corset abandoned in favour of tunic forms in soft drapery. In jewelry, the choker was replaced by the elongated necklace known as the *sautoir* (*see pp. 136-137*). The emphasis had shifted from the *décolleté* to a new column-like silhouette, perfectly complemented by the vertical line of the *sautoir*, a clear demonstration of how decisively a change in the style of dress can transform taste in jewelry.

The *sautoirs* introduced at this time were formed mainly of bands or ropes of woven seed pearls supporting pendants or tassels (*see pp. 142-143*). The favourite gemstones continued to be pearls and diamonds mounted in platinum with *millegrain* setting. The decorative motifs of these new elongated necklaces differed from those of the earlier part of the century, which had been heavily indebted to the Louis Seize style. Fluttering ribbon bows and garlands were replaced by more pronounced geometrical elements. Such *sautoirs* may be viewed as a transitional form of necklace, forerunners of the fashionable *sautoir* of the 1920s. Some exceptional examples were produced, entirely set with diamonds, while others were formed of either fine diamond-set chains or silk cords supporting variously designed pendants.

The Art Deco Years

The outbreak of World War I in 1914 brought the first, frivolous years of the century to an abrupt end. The conflict also brought production of jewelry to a virtual standstill: precious metals and gemstones became scarce; platinum, an important material in the manufacture of nitric acid for explosives and engine magnetos, disappeared from jewelry workshops. Jewelry craftsmen were forced to turn their skills to the armaments industry, while women took the jobs left vacant by men called to the front. They adopted a much more practical style of dress, devoid of corset, looser, shorter and more comfortable, a reflection of their active involvement in working life.

When the fashion industry began to recover in 1919, the simplified dress introduced during the war years was transformed into the fashionable tunic dress of the 1920s. The newly emancipated women strove for an androgynous look, a new boyish appearance characterized by hairstyles *à la garçonne*, shortened dresses and the concealment of feminine curves. Hips and waist disappeared under column-like tunics, which also tended to flatten the chest. In jewelry fashion, the greater verticality of the line of the dress and the flatness of the chest had the effect of promoting the wearing of the *sautoir*. Styles which favour a pronounced bust are undoubtedly better suited to ornaments which fit closely around the neck, while a flat bust calls for long articulated necklaces which can hang and swing freely without impediment. The twenties, then, saw the *sautoir* become the dominant form of necklace, sweeping aside all earlier styles and often worn in combination with very long earrings.

The 1920s *sautoir* differed from those of the previous decade in a number of ways. It was marginally shorter – on average, 80 cm in length (*see pp. 166-167*). In this, it reflected the move towards shorter skirts, which called for shorter chains. The delicacy and intricacy of the earlier examples were replaced by much bolder geometrical patterns and motifs. The new *sautoirs* reflected the fashionable design trends of the time, which were given official if belated recognition at the 1925 Exposition Internationale des Arts Décoratifs et Industriels Modernes in Paris. This event promoted the creation of innovative jewels in the style which came to be known as Art Deco, an abbreviation of the title of the exhibition. These 'modern' *sautoirs* were based on linear geometrical designs, stylized naturalistic decorative elements and gemstones of contrasting colours, echoing the strong chromatic contrasts and geometrical forms in the paintings of the Fauves, Cubists and Futurists in the early part of the century.

The delayed appearance of such a palette in jewelry is partly explicable by the hiatus in production occasioned by World War I and partly by the fact that jewelry, due to its high intrinsic value, can rarely be an experimental medium. The decorative motifs of the Art Deco *sautoirs* were characterized by an extraordinary eclecticism, ranging from pure geometric shapes to stylizations of nature and reinterpretations of exotic Oriental forms and motifs from Ancient Egyptian art. The latter, in particular, came into fashion following the discovery of the treasure of Tutankhamun in 1922. Sphinxes, obelisks, palmettes, lotus flowers, scarabs and hieroglyphs, together with stylized representations of Egyptian divinities, were incorporated into jewelry design. The flat, two-dimensional quality and bright chromatic contrasts of Egyptian art made it an ideal vehicle for the aspirations of Art Deco designers. A number of *sautoirs* of the period also seem to owe something to the decorative arts of India in their use of coloured gemstone beads, and emeralds, sapphires and rubies carved in foliate and floral patterns, reminiscent of Mughal gems. Chinese motifs, such as lanterns and pagodas, also entered the designer's repertoire and frequently featured as pendants on *sautoirs*.

These new, exciting possibilities in jewelry design were embraced with enthusiasm by all the leading Parisian firms – Boucheron, Cartier, Chaumet and Van Cleef & Arpels – whose creations of the period were truly outstanding and justly achieved world-wide fame. Striking chromatic effects were created by unusual combinations of gemstones which had not been previously used in high jewelry. Precious and semiprecious gems were juxtaposed: green jade, black onyx and colourless diamonds or green emeralds, red rubies and blue sapphires and lapis lazuli. Such combinations were made not only with the object of achieving bold colour contrasts but also of emphasizing the different ways gems reflect light. This was achieved by setting semi-translucent jade with glittering diamonds, or opaque onyx with transparent rock crystal. Such adventurous and stylish innovations in design were complemented by innovations in the lapidary field.

Diamonds were cut in more unusual shapes, such as trapezes, semicircles, darts, barrels and triangles. Calibrated coloured precious and semiprecious gems were often given buff tops, which had rarely been used before. The reason for such a development could be found in the new styles – colourful, flat and geometric – which called for a new, compact disposition of the gems, arranged in tightly fitting mosaics, in contrast to the lacy open-work effect of garland-style jewels. This overall compact mosaic effect was further enhanced by extensive use of *pavé* setting, which allowed large surfaces of the jewel to be covered with small gemstones set very close together, concealing to a large degree the supporting metal structure.

The *sautoir* continued to be in vogue into the late 1920s, but with some new features which reflected developments in jewelry fashion (*see pp. 164-165*). Perhaps the most striking innovation of the period was the monochromatic use of diamonds mounted in platinum. The play of colour typical of the earlier part of the decade was replaced by a varied play of light, achieved by juxtaposing diamonds of different cuts and different settings. Commenting on the 1929 exhibition at the Palais Galliera in Paris, jewelry designer Georges Fouquet noted: 'If the 1925 Exposition was characterized by colour, then the keynote at Galliera was certainly white.' In terms of design, stylized naturalistic motifs were displaced by repeated bold geometric patterns, often inspired by industrial and mechanical parts, such as bicycle chains, nuts and bolts. Pendants were given a fuller outline, reminiscent of chandeliers and door-knockers. Sinuous patterns engraved on the side of the metal mounts disappeared along with *millegrain* setting. Another distinguishing feature of these late 1920s *sautoirs* was their versatility. In most cases, the chain divided into sections which could be worn as shorter necklaces or bracelets, while the detachable pendant doubled as a brooch.

Into the Thirties

The 1929 Wall Street Crash brought in its wake a global economic slump. Paradoxically, however, the jewelry industry continued to thrive, jewels becoming larger than ever before and of greater intrinsic value. This can perhaps be explained by the social and economic premium placed on portable precious goods in times of crisis and political and economic instability. Surprisingly, although current fashions promoted a more feminine and curvaceous silhouette than in the 1920s, jewelry design for once did not respond. On the contrary, bold and massive constructions in geometrical patterns came to dominate the market.

The new emphasis on shapely busts made long *sautoirs* unfashionable and short necklaces came back into vogue (*see pp. 168-169*). These were mainly designed as graduated collars of varying width, formed at the front of a festoon of gemstones gathered at each side in a knot, buckle or twist motif. The presence of a decorative element suspended from the clasp at the back was another peculiar feature of these necklaces, though this device *was* related to current dress fashion. Evening gowns of the period

A 1930s advertisement for Van Cleef
& Arpels, Paris, illustrating the fashion
for bare-back dresses with necklaces
embellished with pendants at the back.

were designed to reveal the bare back almost down to the waist and many such dresses
look as if they had been created to be seen from the rear. It is not surprising that jewelers seized on this opportunity to adorn a hitherto neglected part of the body with
pendants, drops and tassels.

The decorative repertoire of these necklaces featured a compact repetition of bold
geometrical motifs, festooned bands, and draped and furled ribbons (*see pp. 174-175*). The
common denominator of such necklaces was their static rather than flowing design.
This did not interfere, however, with a supple and articulated structure, synonymous in
high jewelry with fine-quality workmanship. As the decade wore on, the earlier designs,
distinguished by a marked geometricality, tended to give way to a more fluid approach.
In keeping with the heaviness of such necklaces, the gemstones tended to be large and
used unsparingly. At the beginning of the decade necklaces were usually set entirely
with diamonds, following the trend for white, monochromatic jewelry – a trend which
had appeared already in the late 1920s. By the mid 1930s, however, coloured gems were
once again being lavishly used, at times fashioned *en cabochon*. Judging from the sheer
number of extant examples and contemporary archive records, necklaces in which
rubies were combined with diamonds were especially fashionable. In 1936, the Duke of
Windsor, then Edward VIII, purchased from Van Cleef & Arpels in Paris a fine
Burmese ruby and diamond necklace of *festonné* design, made in 1935, as a gift to mark
Mrs Simpson's 40th birthday (*see pp. 170-171*). Only three years later the Windsors
returned the necklace to the jeweler to have it unset and remodelled into a completely
different style, with a lateral tassel motif. The Duchess, who considered herself a leader

in fashion, almost certainly did not want a necklace so similar in design to those being worn by a great many other fashionable ladies of the day.

Among all coloured gemstones, rubies look especially attractive at night, so it is not surprising that they were chosen for these lavish creations. A fashion editorial of *Excelsior Modes* in 1937, commenting on this combination of rubies and diamonds, noted what a fine display it made under artificial light. The fact that Burmese rubies feature in so many necklaces of the time, as well as in other jewels, suggests an unprecedented availability of this precious and extremely rare material. Again, these necklaces were notable for their versatility. They were constructed in such a way that their decorative elements could be detached and used in a variety of ways: as clips, double clips, bracelet centres, ear clips and head ornaments. One favourite form of doubling was as pairs of lapel clips, among the most fashionable ornaments of the time (*see pp. 170-171*).

The Restrictive Forties

The production of high jewelry came almost to a standstill throughout Europe on the outbreak of World War II. This was partly due to the fact that the general climate of wartime hardly encouraged extravagant display, and partly due to the widespread legislation which was introduced in all European countries to regulate the industry and control the use of precious metals. Platinum was banned from being employed in jewelry production, as it was needed for the armaments industry. The use of gold was restricted, and those wishing to commission a piece of jewelry were required to supply most or all of the raw material. Consequently, jewelry was frequently made of thin, low-carat gold. After forty years in which platinum had reigned supreme, yellow gold became the main feature of the entire jewelry production of the 1940s. At the same time, the irregular supply of gemstones – diamonds from South Africa, and sapphires and rubies from Burma – caused a scarcity on the market. This led to the resetting of gemstones taken from older pieces of jewelry and a widespread use of synthetic rubies and sapphires. When precious stones were used, they were mainly small and relatively inexpensive. Large semiprecious gemstones were favoured: aquamarine, amethyst, citrine and topaz were relatively cheap yet highly effective. In spite of the great difficulties created by the war, jewelry still remained an ideal form of portable capital, and therefore went on being designed, produced and sold.

Although Paris fell to the Germans in 1940, the fashion industry survived, rising to the challenge of limited materials and concentrating on masculine, well-tailored suits and dresses with wide square shoulders reminiscent of military uniforms. Just as couturiers had to adapt to the new circumstances, so did jewelers. The days of grand formal social gatherings and lavish evening gowns adorned by diamonds were over, replaced by less ostentatious events such as cocktail parties, which demanded more practical dresses and gold jewelry set sparingly with gemstones, to reflect the new social austerity. Necklaces, accordingly, were short, since masculine jackets and dresses with square *décolletés* were unsuitable for long forms of neck ornament. Made of gold set with small gemstones, they matched the requirements of the new, more austere life-style throughout Europe and the United States (*see pp. 172-173*). Most necklaces of this time were made of extremely flexible tubular gold bands, arranged in a variety of ways. Among the most common was that of wrapping the band around the neck and tying it in a knot, sometimes secured with decorative motifs such as flowers and ribbon bows. The use of a single or double band around the neck, applied with a variety of decorative motifs, was also popular, occasionally further enhanced by tassel motifs.

The flexible tubular bands were of two types. The first, commonly known as the snake chain, consisted of a succession of tightly interlocking gold links of different shapes; its overall effect was sinuous and serpent-like, hence the name. The second type was known as gas-pipe linking, due to its resemblance to the tube of a petrol pump or a gas hose (*see pp. 178-179*). It was formed of two long strips of gold with raised edges tightly wrapped around a removable core; these strips interlocked with one another and required no soldering. The famous *passe-partout* necklace created by Van Cleef & Arpels in 1939 maximized the potential of gas-pipe linking. It was formed of a long tubular band which could be wrapped around the neck in a variety of ways and secured by a gem-set floral clip. This necklace also doubled as a bracelet or belt when wrapped around the wrist or waist, a good illustration of the innovative, decorative and versatile responses to the scarcity of materials in the 1940s.

The 'New Look' Fifties

The relatively strong economic boom which followed the war and the desire to rebuild and restore what had been destroyed brought a new prosperity to the early 1950s. Western economies flourished and a self-conscious consumerism began to emerge. In fashion, there was a movement to replace the stiff, masculine cuts of the wartime years with a more feminine silhouette. This inspired narrow-waisted and puff-skirt dresses, based on the crinoline of the 1860s. After periods of prolonged social and economic crisis, fashion often tends towards sumptuousness and the nostalgic revival of past trends. Couturiers, in particular, indulged in a profusion of luxury fabrics, such as silks and satins, lace and brocades. This trend reached its apogee in Christian Dior's spring collection of 1947, christened the 'New Look' by Carmel Snow, editor-in-chief of *Harper's Bazaar*. Dior, describing the spirit behind his new collection, spoke for the age: 'We were emerging from a time of war, of uniforms, and of women soldiers built like boxers. I designed flower-like women, with delicate shoulders, blossoming bosoms, narrow liana-like waists and skirts as wide as corollas.... I wanted my dresses to be built and moulded round the curves of a woman's body and to stylise its contours. I accentuated the waists and the volume of the hips; I set off the bust to its best advantage.'

On such 'New Look' busts, often accentuated by extra padding, short necklaces were displayed to their best advantage, and indeed became immensely fashionable.

(*continued on p. 193*)

A BOUCHERON CHOKER

This spectacular diamond choker (*above*) by Boucheron, 1899, exemplifies neck ornament in the early 20th century at its most lavish. Sometimes referred to as *résille* or *draperie de décolleté*, it consists of a wide band tightly encircling the neck, with additional decoration extending down the *décolleté* and entirely encrusted with precious gems, usually diamonds.

THE 'DOG COLLAR'

Chokers continued to be the fashionable necklace type during the early years of the 20th century. The wide bands, closely hugging the neck, were realized in a variety of materials, and were sometimes referred to as *colliers de chien*, due to their resemblance to dog collars. There were, however, a number of variations to this fashionable type: one consisted of a shaped gem-set plaque fitted either to strands of pearls or black fabric; another variation consisted of a band entirely strung with pearls or set with gemstones.

The magnificent example *(right)* by Cartier, Paris, 1907, has a central motif in platinum and diamonds strung on eighteen rows of seed pearls which can be detached and secured to an alternative black velvet choker or worn separately as a brooch. Another choker *(below)* by Cartier, Paris, made in 1906, is encrusted throughout with diamonds. Both these examples are mounted in platinum and the stones held in *millegrain* settings, whereby the platinum around the stone is beaded to create a more 'frothy' and lace-like effect. Their design, which relies on the use of foliate garland motifs, is yet another typical feature and a trademark of Cartier at this time.

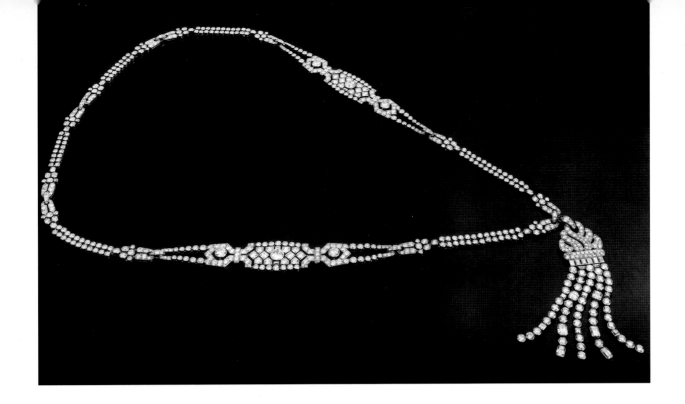

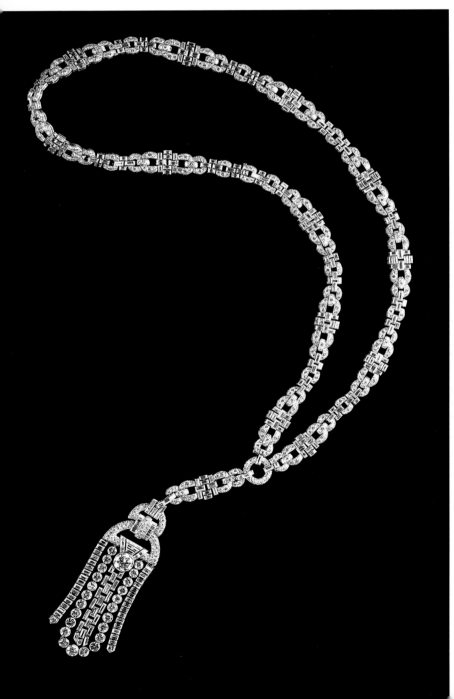

Two diamond *sautoirs* (*above* and *left*) by Van Cleef & Arpels, Paris, made in 1927 and 1928 respectively, and a diamond *sautoir* (*below*) by Boucheron, Paris, 1930–31; *sautoirs* continued to be in vogue well into the late 1920s. These later examples may be distinguished from those of the earlier years of the decade by their monochromatic use of diamonds mounted in platinum, which replaced earlier strong and contrasting colour combinations, and by the repetition of bold geometric motifs often inspired by industrial and mechanical parts. Pendants were given a fuller outline, reminiscent of chandeliers or even door-knockers.

INTO THE JAZZ AGE

The 1920s saw the *sautoir* become the dominant form of necklace, often worn in combination with very long earrings. Its elongated line beautifully complemented the verticality of the line of contemporary dress illustrated in these contemporary fashion photographs. Madame Renée Puissant (*below*) was the daughter of Alfred Van Cleef; on the death of her husband Émile in 1926, she became artistic director of the family firm where she collaborated with designer René-Sim Lacaze. Viscountess Wimborne (*right*) was the wife of one of the richest men in England, and well-known for her style and beauty. Marion Moorhouse (*below right*) was photographed in 1929 in New York for *Vogue*. Both photographs are by Cecil Beaton.

Another distinguishing feature of late 1920s *sautoirs* was their versatility. The chain could be divided into sections to be worn as shorter necklaces or as bracelets, while the detachable pendant often doubled as a brooch. In this French diamond *sautoir* (*left*), *c.* 1930, it is worth noting the characteristic use of diamonds of different shapes, rather than coloured gems, and the repetition of geometric patterns, inspired in this instance by bicycle chains.

THE ECLECTIC *SAUTOIR*

Sautoirs of the mid 1920s were based on linear geometrical designs characterized by strongly contrasting colour combinations and an extraordinary eclecticism, ranging from geometric shapes to stylizations of nature, reinterpretations of exotic Oriental forms, and motifs from Ancient Egyptian art, which began to influence fashion after the discovery of the treasures of Tutankhamun in 1922. This carved emerald, black enamel and diamond *sautoir* (*above*) is by Mauboussin, Paris, *c*. 1927; note the use of the carved coloured gemstones in the Mughal way.

This ruby and diamond *sautoir* (*left*) by Cartier, Paris, 1927, has a detachable pendant clearly inspired by a Chinese lantern motif. The emerald, ruby, onyx and diamond Egyptian-design *sautoir* by Van Cleef & Arpels, Paris, 1924, is shown here together with its original stock card design (*opposite*).

SHORT NECKLACES OF THE THIRTIES

During the 1930s short necklaces came back into vogue largely as a consequence of a change in the style of dress which called for a much more curvaceous female silhouette. Many necklaces were constructed in such a way that their decorative elements could be detached and used in a variety of roles: as dress clips, double-clip brooches, bracelet centres, ear clips and head ornaments.

This platinum and diamond necklace (*opposite above*) by Cartier, London, *c.* 1935, makes an overall monochromatic effect, while the marked geometricality of the design is especially characteristic of the early 1930s. The reverse (*opposite below*) illustrates how five of the triangular elements may be detached and either worn separately or as a double-clip brooch on an attachment or as terminals on the white gold and black enamel bangle.

The diamond necklace (*right*), *c.* 1938, has a more fluid design of scrolled ribbon motifs, a fashionable device of the mid to late 1930s. The reverse illustrates its versatility: on an appropriate fitting it may be worn upside down as a tiara; the four central elements can be detached and the larger ones worn as dress clips and the smaller as ear clips.

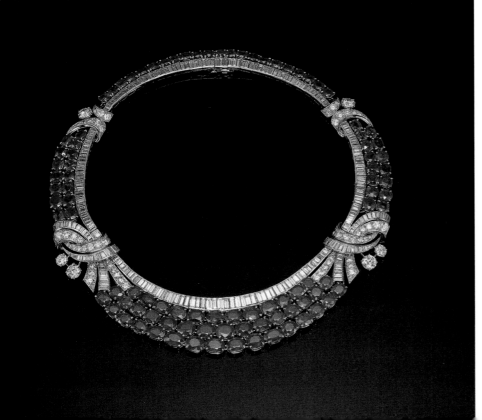

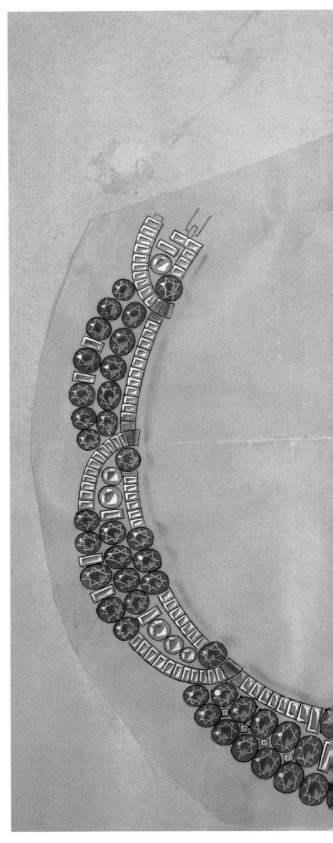

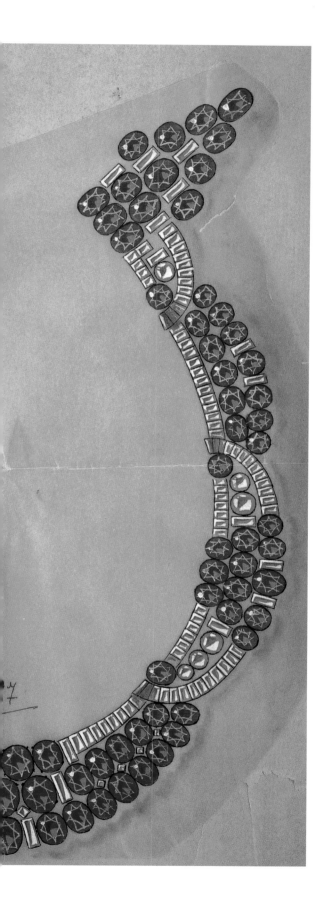

THE RETURN OF THE RUBY

By the middle years of the decade, colour had once again come to be a feature of jewelry design. The combination of fine Burmese rubies and diamonds emerged as the dominant pairing in fashionable design, usually in the form of a single or multiple festoon, as illustrated by examples on these pages. The cushion-shaped Burmese ruby and baguette diamond necklace (*opposite above left*) is probably by Van Cleef & Arpels, Paris. A similar combination of gemstones can be observed in a cushion-shaped ruby and baguette and brilliant-cut diamond necklace (*opposite below left*).

This archive design (*left*) from Van Cleef & Arpels, is of the famous ruby and diamond necklace of 1935 given by the future Duke of Windsor to Mrs Wallis Simpson on the occasion of her 40th birthday in 1936. Note the decorative motif suspended from the clasp. This necklace was redesigned in 1939 by René-Sim Lacaze of Van Cleef & Arpels in a more daring style to satisfy the fashion-conscious Windsors. *Cabochon* rubies and baguette and brilliant-cut diamonds combine again in this French necklace (*above*).

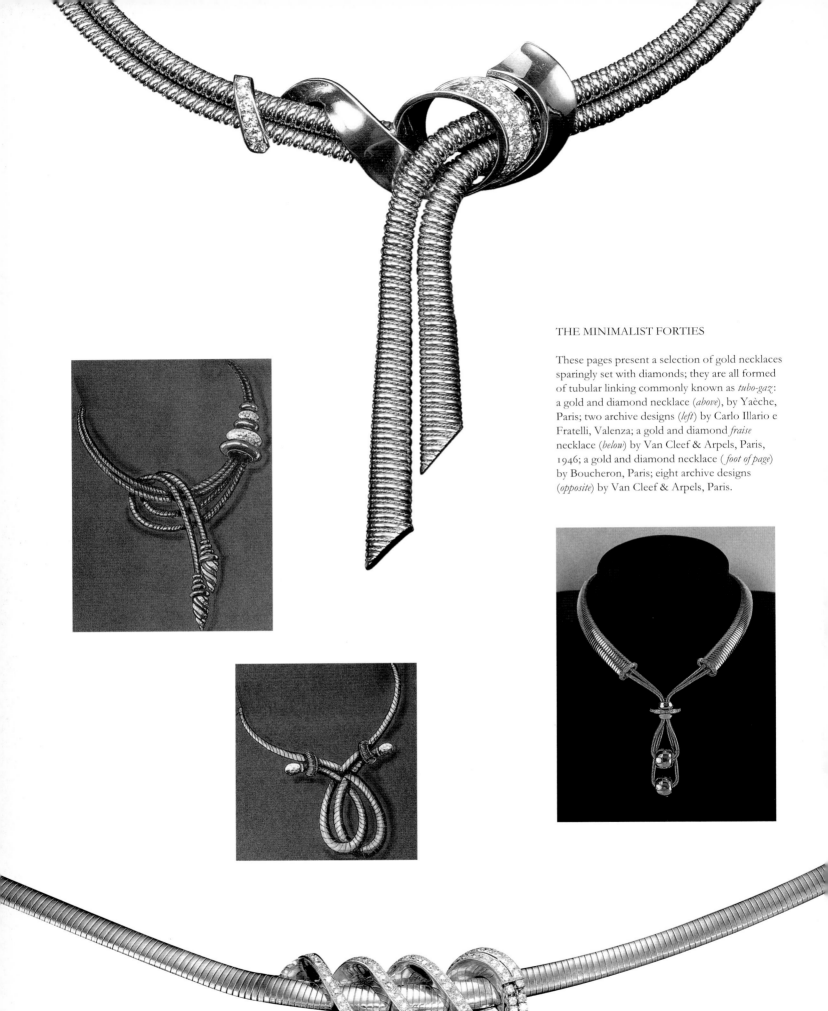

THE MINIMALIST FORTIES

These pages present a selection of gold necklaces sparingly set with diamonds; they are all formed of tubular linking commonly known as *tubo-gaz*: a gold and diamond necklace (*above*), by Yaèche, Paris; two archive designs (*left*) by Carlo Illario e Fratelli, Valenza; a gold and diamond *fraise* necklace (*below*) by Van Cleef & Arpels, Paris, 1946; a gold and diamond necklace (*foot of page*) by Boucheron, Paris; eight archive designs (*opposite*) by Van Cleef & Arpels, Paris.

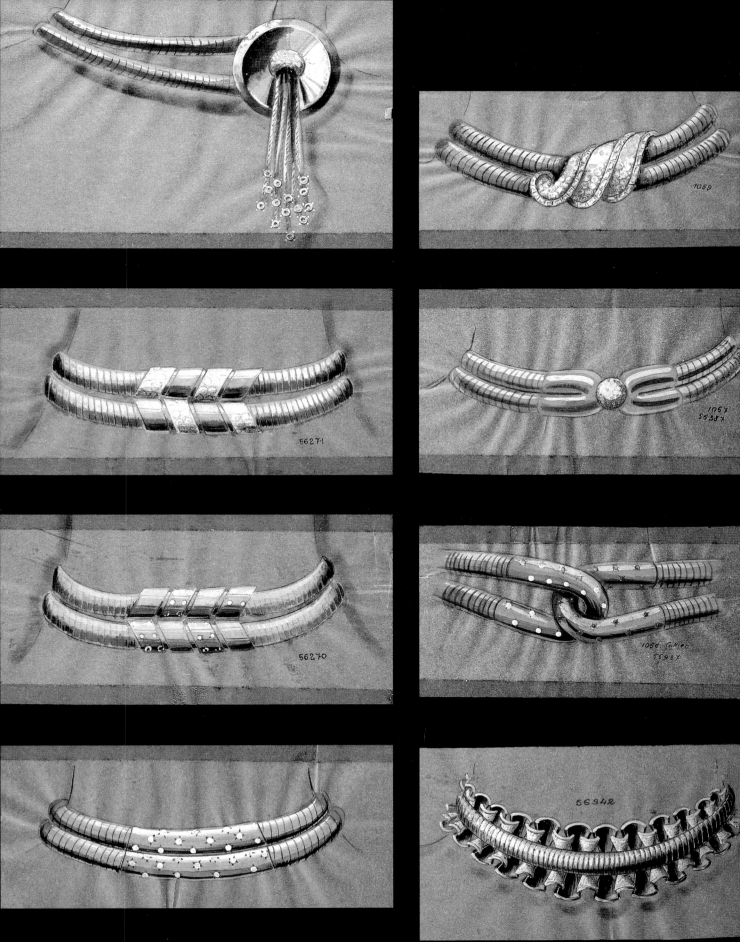

EMERALDS, SAPPHIRES AND DIAMONDS

The dominant feature of 1930s necklaces was their bold design, with large gemstones lavishly set in platinum. Their common denominator was a static rather than a flowing design, though the actual structure was supple and articulated, as is immediately evident in these superb examples, including this fine Colombian *cabochon* emerald and diamond necklace (*left*), *c.* 1935; the detachable front may be worn as a bracelet.

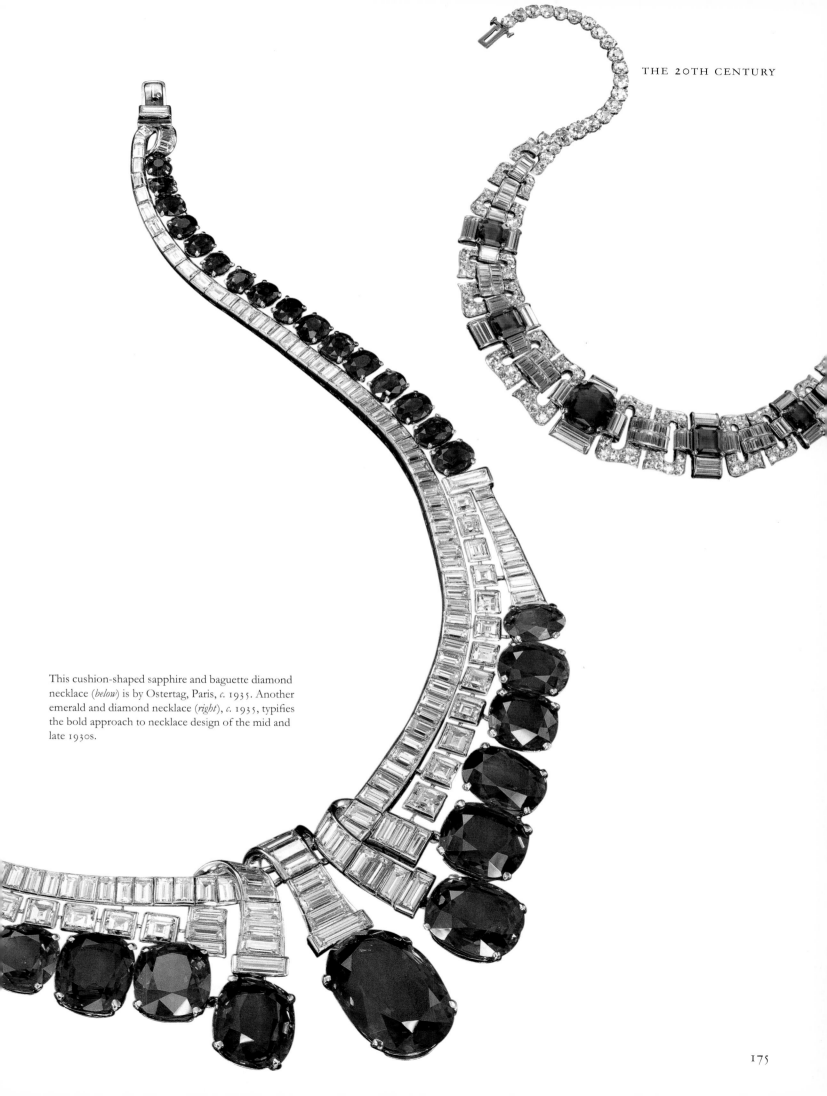

This cushion-shaped sapphire and baguette diamond necklace (*below*) is by Ostertag, Paris, *c.* 1935. Another emerald and diamond necklace (*right*), *c.* 1935, typifies the bold approach to necklace design of the mid and late 1930s.

THE AFTERNOON NECKLACE

In the 1950s, at the same time as the resurgence of sumptuous diamond necklaces, gold necklaces set either with small diamonds or coloured stones were gaining popularity as a complement to the fashionable afternoon dress. Their overall design resembled that of the diamond models: curvilinear, fluid, asymmetrical and extremely feminine. But they were distinguished by an extraordinarily varied and imaginative rendering of the gold, worked into fabric-like patterns, as if the jeweler was challenging the couturier in reproducing the opulent feel of textiles.

Some necklaces were even designed as knotted cravats: the necklace (*above left*) by Van Cleef & Arpels, Paris, 1951, has gold-work which simulates crochet and is fastened by an emerald bead button and diamond-set eye; the gold *foulard* necklace (*above right*) by Boucheron, Paris, 1954, is decorated with ninety-eight small *cabochon* rubies and interchangeable central clusters respectively set with a *cabochon* turquoise and with diamonds.

The design for the gold *collier fermeture éclaire* (zip necklace) (*far left*), decorated with small rubies and diamonds, was created by Van Cleef & Arpels, Paris, as early as 1939, but only really came into its own in the early 1950s. This piece dates from 1951; it is an extreme example of the fashionable trend of designing gold necklaces to simulate fabric trimmings. With the zipper closed (*left*), the necklace could be transformed into a bracelet.

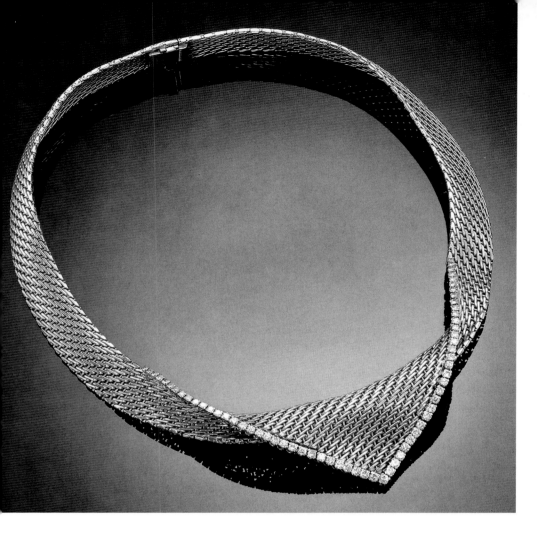

This woven gold necklace (*above*) by Asprey, London, 1959, has a front decorated with brilliant-cut diamonds. Another fine example of the 1950s short necklace imitating clothing is this French gold basket-weave necklace (*right*), designed as a knotted scarf studded with cushion-shaped diamonds.

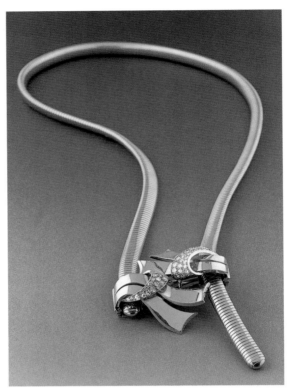

VAN CLEEF & ARPELS

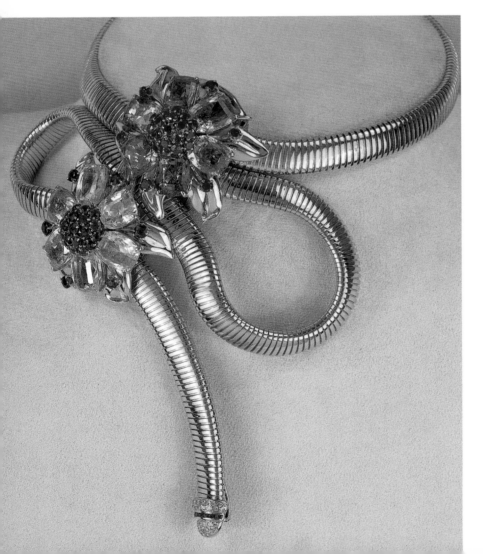

MERLE OBERON

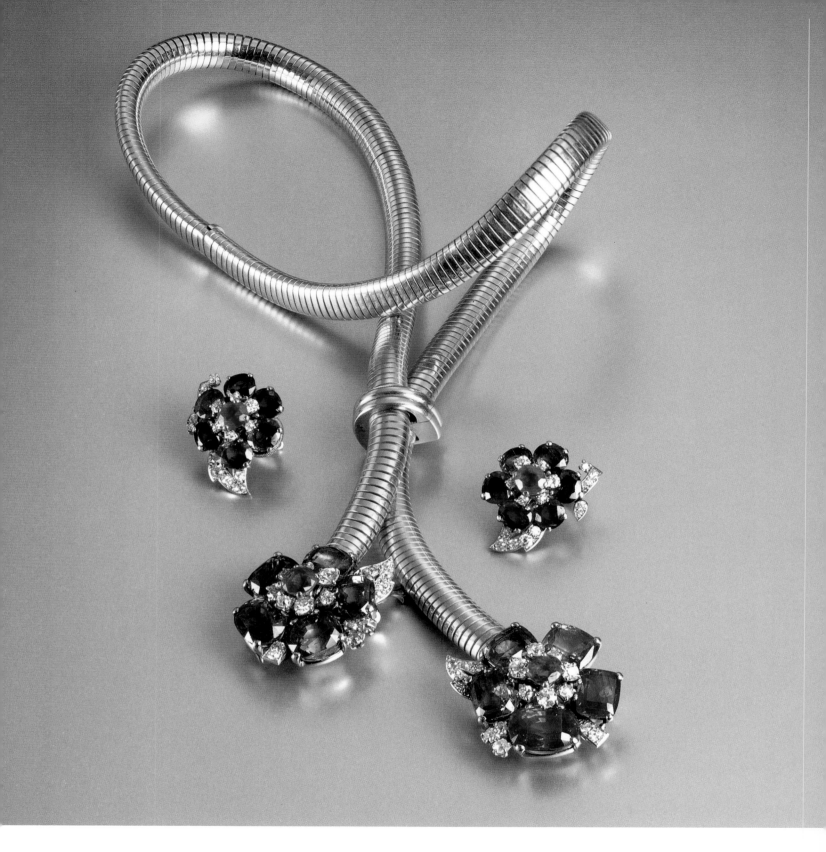

'GAS-PIPE' LINKING

These examples of gold and gem-set short necklaces of the 1940s illustrate the supple
and versatile nature of 'gas-pipe' linking. This gold, ruby, sapphire and diamond necklace
(*above*) by Cartier, London, 1945, has a detachable flowerhead cluster *en suite* with the
earclips which can be worn separately as dress clips. The gold 'gas-pipe' necklace (*opposite
above*) has detachable scroll-shaped clips decorated with diamonds set in platinum, by Van
Cleef & Arpels, Paris, 1943. The gold, yellow and pale blue sapphire *passe-partout* necklace
(*opposite below*), also by Van Cleef & Arpels, 1939, is especially fine; it was prominently
displayed in the firm's contemporary advertisements, one of which featured the actress
Merle Oberon.

THE 'NEW LOOK' FIFTIES

Short necklaces lavishly set with diamonds were the ultimate fashionable neck ornament for evening wear during the 1950s; they complemented perfectly the deep *décolleté* of 'New Look' silk, lace and brocade evening gowns. All designs are characterized by a distinctively fluid and asymmetrical outline, achieved largely through 'channel' setting.

The style is well illustrated in this advertisement (*above*) for Boucheron, 1955, and in this French necklace (*above right*) lavishly set with diamonds, *c.* 1955, supporting at one side a characteristic flowing cascade motif. An American example of the style is this platinum and diamond necklace (*below*) by Harry Winston, New York, 1950, designed as an asymmetrical collar formed of a *rivière* of brilliant-cut diamonds flanked by two rows of baguette-shaped diamonds in a 'channel' setting to achieve a smooth and continuous outline. Another advertisement (*opposite*) for Boucheron, 1958, illustrates the fashionable diamond festoon necklaces of the time; these examples divide to form bracelets, but can also be made more precious by adding an extra *rivière*.

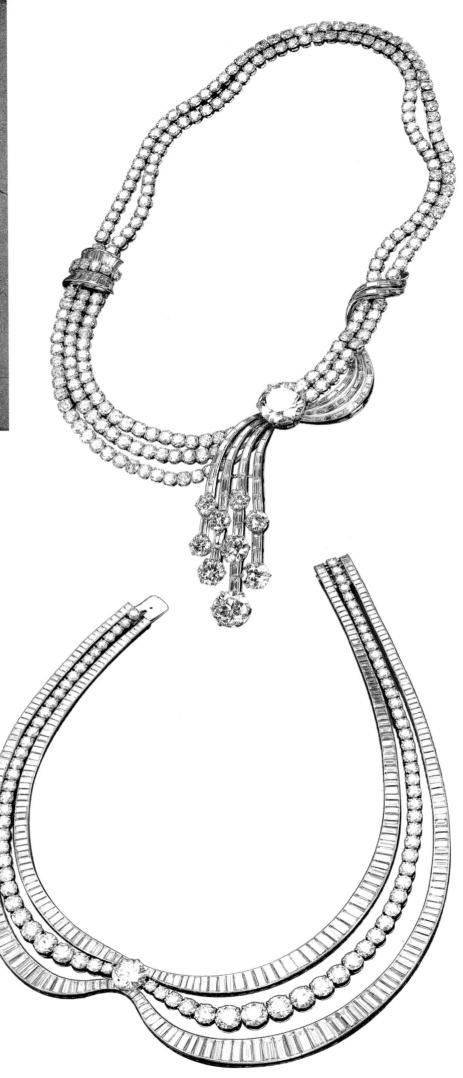

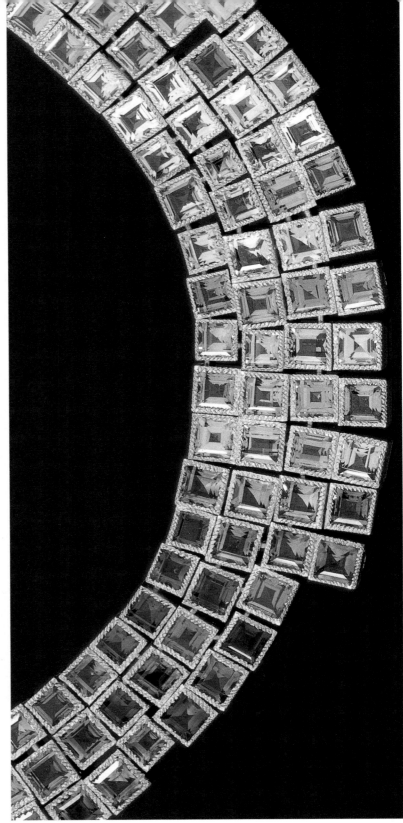

ICONOCLASM IN THE SIXTIES AND EARLY SEVENTIES

This necklace (*top left* and *detail above right*) by Andrew Grima, London, 1970, is set with tourmalines, aquamarines, peridots, citrines, amethysts and tanzanites in textured gold mounts. Another example by the same jeweler (*centre left* and *detail below left*), set with sixty-eight triangular citrines and forty-one diamonds in gold, dates from 1974. This 1960s piece (*opposite*) is a fine example of the work of Gilbert Albert of Geneva; it is set with chalcedony nodules, cultured baroque pearls and diamonds in gold.

SHORT NECKLACES OF THE SIXTIES

Necklaces of high intrinsic value created in the 1960s by the established jewelry firms followed the trend for abstraction set by the artist jewelers. The most typical designs consisted of stylized garlands of floral motifs characterized by dynamic outlines and fairly restrained asymmetry. These were often rendered with broken jagged contours, achieved by alternating circular-cut gems with pointed marquise- and pear-shaped stones. This diamond necklace (*below*), set with marquise- and brilliant-cut diamonds, is a typical example of the time and very similar to the necklace worn by Mrs Alfred Bloomingdale in her portrait photograph by Cecil Beaton (*right*).

In this design by Milanese jeweler Faraone for a *cabochon* sapphire and diamond necklace, the spiky, thorn-like contours typical of the 1960s are accentuated by a form of setting which consisted of securing the stone in prominent beaded prongs of white metal, clearly seen in this design.

The two necklaces (*right*) by Milanese jeweler Cusi of Via Montenapoleone are respectively set with emeralds and diamonds, and rubies and diamonds; their asymmetry and jagged contours, obtained by the juxtaposition of rounded and pointed stones mounted in beaded prong settings, are typical of the decade.

Br. 2836
Pend. 55889

Br. 2442

NEPAL

N° 55986

Many features of the 1970s *sautoir* are indebted to Indian art in general and Indian jewelry in particular. Decorative motifs of Mughal inspiration, with vibrant colour combinations of green, red and white, typical of Jaipur enamel-work, and coloured gemstones cut *en cabochon*, were often incorporated in the long chains of this period.

This spectacular ruby, emerald and diamond *sautoir* by David Webb, New York, is a good example of this trend. As was the case with all *sautoirs* of the period, irrespective of the type and quality of the gems and even including those lavishly set with diamonds, this example is made of yellow gold. This combination represented a real break with tradition; since the 18th century diamonds had always been set in white metal to increase their own whiteness. This shift in taste was born very much from the desire to render jewelry more wearable during the day.

THE SEVENTIES: THE RETURN OF THE LONG NECKLACE

After four decades of short necklaces, long chains came back into fashion in the 1970s, often formed either of beads or variously shaped links carved in hardstone or unusual materials such as exotic woods or tortoiseshell, and frequently supporting large detachable pendants *(opposite above left)*. Vibrant colours featured prominently: black onyx and green chalcedony, turquoise and lapis lazuli, blue topaz or yellow citrine, for instance. This *sautoir (opposite right)* by Kutchinsky, London, is made of carved onyx, pink coral, gold and diamonds. The two designs *(opposite below left)* for carved hardstone and diamond *sautoirs* are by Boucheron, Paris, 1976.

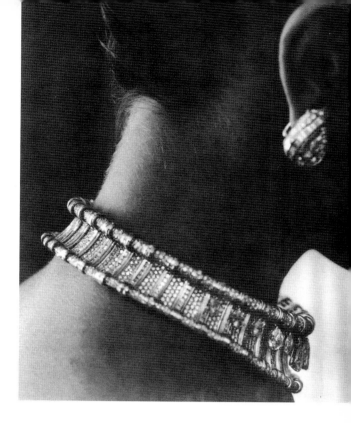

THE EMANCIPATED EIGHTIES

The executive woman of the 1980s required practical neck ornaments which had to be decorative, but also easy to wear. During the 1980s and early 1990s single strands of exceptionally large cultured pearls known as South Sea, worn hugging the base of the neck, were at the height of fashion. The pearls were extremely decorative and extremely precious - large and regularly-shaped specimens are very rare - but were also very practical and could be worn from morning until night, or from the boardroom to the opera.

These three exceptionally fine single-strand South Sea cultured pearl necklaces (*opposite* and *left*) date from the late 1980s and early 1990s: a strand (*opposite above left*) with twenty-five cultured pearls graduated from 18.7 mm in diameter to 15 mm, the clasp set with a step-cut diamond of 15.10 carats; a strand (*opposite below left*) with twenty-three pearls graduated from approximately 20 mm in diameter to 16 mm, the clasp set with a circular-cut diamond of 11.80 carats; a strand (*left*) with twenty-nine natural black colour cultured pearls graduated from approximately 17 mm to 13 mm, on a diamond-set clasp. This yellow gold and diamond necklace (*below*) by Bulgari, Rome, 1989, has a fringe of pear-shaped stones, weighing 45.37 carats, contained within the concave structure of the collar. A similar collar is shown in the advertisement by Bulgari (*above*), 1989.

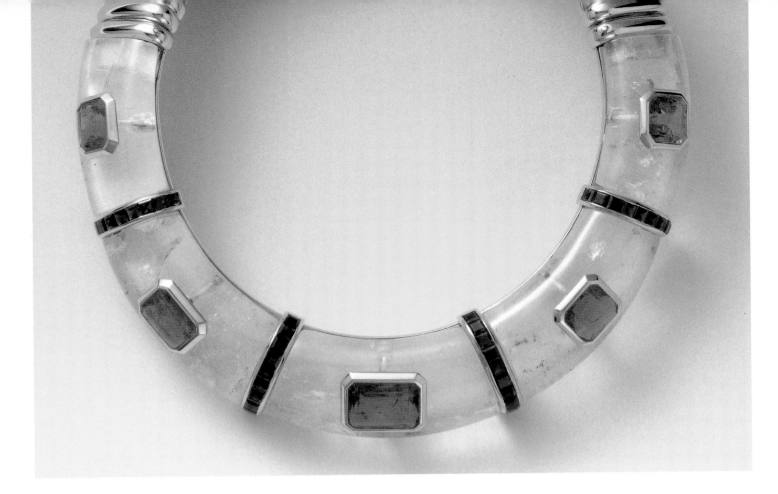

POWER DRESSING

Collars worn at the base of the neck were the preferred form of necklace of the 1980s. They were both decorative and at the same time easy to wear, consisting usually of a wide convex band of metal and gemstones, which perfectly complemented the tailored, structured line of contemporary dress. The outlines were neat and controlled, while decoration was largely a play of rounded geometrical motifs; even when naturalistic elements were included, they were stylized and contained within a geometrical framework.

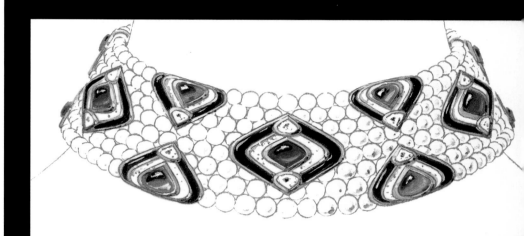

When penannular, these collars were fitted with springs to allow them to encircle the neck snugly, as in these four designs (*right*) in yellow gold set with multicoloured gemstones by Marina B, dating respectively (*top to foot of page*) from 1982, 1983, 1987 and 1989. The two gold penannular collars (*opposite*) by Poiray, 1980s, are set respectively with rock crystal, emeralds and sapphires, and mother-of-pearl, rubies, diamonds and a large sapphire; note, in both instances, the geometrical decorative motifs and characteristically neat, sleek outline.

Overleaf: The 1980s saw a revival of the limited production of lavish, expensive necklaces set with very rare stones.

The diamond necklace illustrated, by Harry Winston, New York, 1986, is an exceptionally fine example of this type of creation. Set with 139.32 carats of diamonds, the front supports ten pear-shaped diamonds of the finest quality (D colour, internally flawless) weighing a total of 99.34 carats. Characteristically, all the diamonds are held by very unobtrusive platinum claws which serve a purely functional role.

This necklace was sold at auction in New York in 1994, when it fetched $4, 402, 500 - the record then for any item of jewelry sold at auction.

As *the* personal ornament of the decade, they abandoned the straight, angular lines of Art Deco and the bulky forms of the 1940s, evolving into light, curving and flowing shapes which created a strong impression of movement. This trend is best typified by the lavishly set diamond necklaces of the period, designed specifically for evening wear (*see pp. 180-181*). In their simplest form, these consisted of *rivières* set with brilliant- or baguette-cut diamonds supporting free flowing fringes, supple festoons, or asymmetrical, lateral cascades of variously shaped gems. This basic design could be adapted in many ways and enriched by additional decorative features such as fluttering ribbons, florets and draped motifs. The necklace could be made more precious by the addition of larger and more costly gems: more brilliant-cut diamond *rivières*, for example, more *marquise*-shaped diamond fringes, or more pear-shaped pendant drops. In 1958 Boucheron advertised necklaces which could also be worn as bracelets and enriched with additional diamond-set motifs at any time.

The overall design of these 1950s creations, incorporating lavish displays of gemstones, is reminiscent of the necklaces of the late 1930s. In their efforts to reintroduce a feeling of opulence, jewelers were inevitably drawn to the pre-war years, the last period of extravagance in jewelry. But if late 1930s diamond-set necklaces look similar to those of the 1950s at first glance, closer inspection reveals in the latter a much more fluid and asymmetrical outline and a different approach to the setting. To achieve this fluid line jewelers made considerable use of the 'channel' setting. This entailed setting gemstones, usually baguette-shaped diamonds, in rail-like mounts which provided a continuous, smooth outline. The metal used in these important creations for formal evening wear was invariably white. Platinum made its reappearance, and white gold was widely used; palladium, the lightest metal of the platinum group, was also introduced. Advances in metallurgy led to the creation of white gold and palladium alloys which could be used as alternatives to platinum (*see pp. 180-181*).

Diamonds again reigned supreme during the 1950s. As early as 1948, the De Beers Diamond Corporation, the world's largest producer of diamonds, had started to promote its product with the now famous slogan, 'A Diamond is For Ever'. In June 1951 the French edition of *Vogue* published an article on the latest jewelry with the uncompromising claim, 'the diamond is King'. Its reputation was further enhanced by the song, 'Diamonds are a Girl's Best Friend', sung by Marilyn Monroe in the 1953 film, *Gentlemen Prefer Blondes*. The glittering sparkle of these gems was a happy match for the rich brocades, embroidered silks, and precious laces of contemporary evening gowns, and an ideal complement to the mink coat, then the height of fashion. Although overshadowed by the popularity of diamonds, stones such as emeralds, rubies and sapphires were often used to add a touch of colour to otherwise monochromatic evening creations.

At the same time as the resurgence of sumptuous diamond necklaces, gold necklaces set either with small diamonds or coloured gems were gaining substantially in popularity (*see pp. 176-177*). Their overall design resembled that of the diamond models:

A portrait photograph of Maria Callas by Cecil Beaton, 1957, showing the singer wearing a six-row pearl necklace.

curvilinear, fluid, asymmetrical and extremely feminine. But they were distinguished by an extraordinarily varied and imaginative rendering of the gold. This was worked into pleats, ruffs and passementeries, or woven or fretted into fabric-like patterns, as if the jeweler was challenging the couturier by reproducing the opulent feel of textiles in gold. Terms such as *tissu milanais*, *tissu serge*, *tissu jersey* and *macramé* were used to describe the gold-work of such jewels. An extreme manifestation of this trend was the 'Collier Fermeture Éclaire' (zip necklace) by Van Cleef & Arpels; first designed in 1939, it had become all the rage by the early 1950s. It was constructed in the same manner as a zipper, but in precious metal. The most common examples were in yellow gold, at times embellished with various gemstones. When the zip was open the jewel was worn as a necklace; when closed with a sliding device decorated with a tassel, it became a bracelet. For the latter use, a section could be removed to reduce the length. Other necklaces were designed as cravats, the gold-work simulating crochet and fastened by gem-set eyes and buttons. Even when the gold was not simulating passementerie or fabric, it was characteristically broken up into very fine filaments or corded wire. This rendering was in complete contrast to that of 1940s necklaces, which had incorporated large surfaces of unbroken gold in the place of ostentatious display of gemstones. A consequence of so much intricate gold-work was the extreme flexibility and suppleness of the resulting jewel, features emphasized by Boucheron in an advertising campaign of 1951: 'Boucheron has created this gold ornament whose suppleness matches so gracefully the rounded shape of neck and wrist.' These gold creations were the ideal complement to the elegant afternoon dresses which were the *dernier cri* of fashion designers in the winter of 1952, providing a highly decorative alternative to the lavish diamond-set necklaces of the grand *soirées*.

The decade also witnessed the resurgence of pearls, both natural and cultured. Besides the single strand, necklaces formed of festoons of pearls, gathered at both sides with diamond-set motifs, were among the most fashionable designs – Grace Kelly received such a necklace as a wedding gift from Prince Rainier of Monaco in 1956. Although the great Parisian jewelry houses continued to rival each other in the 1950s, fine design was no longer limited to France. Just as the focus of fashion had begun to move away from Paris to other countries, particularly Italy and the United States, fine, up-to-date jewelry design was beginning to be created by firms such as Bulgari in Italy and Harry Winston in the United States.

Above A pearl and diamond necklace with matching ear clips, ring and bracelet, Van Cleef & Arpels, New York; this was Grace Kelly's wedding gift from Prince Rainier of Monaco.

The Restless Sixties

The well-being and economic stability rediscovered in the 1950s was again called into question in the 1960s. Social disturbance and a tendency to reject the established order on the part of the younger generation were reflected in all the applied arts, including fashion and jewelry design.

One notable example of this was the appearance of the mini skirt. The opulent elegance of Dior's New Look was swept away: rounded hips and prominent busts were substituted by a waif-like silhouette epitomized by the model Twiggy; in the words of James Laver, 'If the psychologist's theory of the Shifting Erogenous Zone can be accepted, once a focus of interest loses its appeal another has to be found.' And, in the early 1960s, the emphasis shifted from the bust to the legs which, in the short skirts of Mary Quant, were universally bared as never before in fashion, while busts returned to a 1920s flatness.

In spite of these changes in fashion, however, necklaces did not notably change in shape from the previous decade; they remained short, designed to encircle the neck (*see pp. 184-185*). The reason for this is almost certainly that, although *sautoirs* would have suited the flat chests of contemporary fashion, they did not suit the proportions of the short dress. Even in an era when the convention was to be unconventional, a necklace longer than the hem-line of the dress was obviously not deemed attractive!

If the form of the 1960s necklace was similar to that of the 1950s, its detailed design was certainly not. On the contrary, necklaces were characterized by innovative render-

Below A portrait photograph of Merle Oberon by Cecil Beaton, 1963, showing the actress wearing a short pearl necklace.

ings reminiscent of organic forms, such as sprawling roots, or amorphous shapes which evoked the moon's surface or the sea bed (*see pp. 182-183*). Nature was transformed by abstraction and stylization into purely decorative forms. Other necklaces were entirely abstract in design, formed of geometrical shapes often arranged in a random yet coherent asymmetrical disposition. The British designer Andrew Grima and Gilbert Albert from Switzerland were foremost among the young jewelers who best captured the spirit of the age.

In the 1960s climate of iconoclasm, it is not surprising that jewelers favoured unusual materials and unconventional ways of working them. Gold, in particular, was sometimes treated in an almost irreverent manner, being textured to achieve rough, rugged, stony effects. At times it appears as an agglomerate of drops and dribbles, as if droplets of the molten metal had been frozen in place. The jury of the 1966 Duke of Edinburgh Prize for Elegant Design reported, 'There is a much less inhibited attitude to new techniques, such as melting under controlled temperatures and new ways of giving different textures to gold. These have given much greater scope to the designer and have released him from the rigid convention of setting.' More than white gold or platinum, yellow gold was especially suitable for this type of rendering.

Gemstones and other materials were selected for their decorative potential rather than intrinsic value. Jewelers made use of uncut gemstones and crystals in their original shapes. The appeal was their irregularity, a feature up to then unexploited in jewelry. Striking and novel effects were often obtained by combining uncut and faceted stones, such as aggregates of amethyst and dioptase or chalcedony nodules, with highly reflective diamonds and shimmering pearls. When precious coloured gemstones were used, they were frequently fashioned *en cabochon*. Their smooth reflective surface provided the sought-after contrast, both in colour and in texture, with the rough gold.

Necklaces of high intrinsic value, created by the established jewelry firms, followed suit, but in a more restrained manner (*see p. 185*). No longer concerned with symmetry and balance, jewelers favoured necklaces designed as stylized garlands of flowers and leaves, another typical example of 1960s abstraction from nature. Such designs were characteristically rendered with broken jagged contours, achieved by alternating circular-cut gems with pointed marquise- and pear-shaped stones. These contorted, thorn-like outlines were further accentuated by a form of setting which consisted of securing the stone in prominent beaded prongs of white metal, usually gold, in strict contrast to the smooth, flowing channel setting typical of the 1950s. Diamonds, the pre-eminent gemstones, continued to be as popular as ever, but emeralds, rubies and sapphires came to be used more prominently. Though the differentiation between high jewelry and humbler jewels, mounted with less precious gems, is still evident, nonetheless there is a common denominator. They both share abstract designs and jagged contours. One interesting point about jewelry in the 1960s is that, in keeping with the anti-establishment spirit of the times, it was the individual artist-designer who set the trends, not the great houses.

Spirituality and Nostalgia in the Seventies

The rampant economic growth of the 1960s began to peter out in the early 1970s, when the oil crisis in the Middle East gave Western economies a violent bout of hyperinflation. By the end of the 1960s the social, moral and cultural revolt of that decade had lost its bite and impetus; attitudes became more tempered and sober. Economic recession engendered a widespread feeling of uncertainty, instability and, inevitably, escapism. Reassurance was sought in exotic spiritual practices and cultures; those of the Indian sub-continent, in particular, satisfied these aspirations, since it was perceived to be relatively uncontaminated by the vices of the West. Reassurance was also sought by a nostalgic look to the past, a sure accompaniment to an overall sense of crisis.

This situation was clearly reflected in contemporary fashion, which began to draw inspiration from ethnic sources and from a distinctly romantic vision of the past. Indian prints, caftans, fringed shawls, gypsy-like full skirts and boleros characterized the first; ruffled blouses, crushed velvets and lace reminiscent of nineteenth-century lingerie were typical of the second. Both styles had in common a fluid, deconstructed silhouette of flowing tops and long skirts.

These changes in fashion inevitably dictated an equally visible change in jewelry, and necklaces in particular. Away went short necklaces which had been the dominant form since the 1930s, to be replaced by long swinging chain necklaces, the ideal complement to the flowing lines of contemporary dress (*see pp. 186-187*). The *sautoirs* of the time were formed either of beads or of a succession of elongated links; these were mostly oval- or lozenge-shaped and supported large, often detachable pendants, conceived either as tassels or as larger versions of one of the elements of the *sautoir*. Not surprisingly, many features of 1970s *sautoirs* were indebted to Indian art in general and Indian jewelry in particular. Arabesque motifs of Mughal inspiration, for instance, made their appearance, as well as vibrant colour combinations of green, red and white derived from the palette of traditional Jaipur enamel-work. Vibrant colours featured prominently, since they complemented contemporary colourful ethnic fashions. Their chromatic effect was achieved by using a variety of materials, from hard to semiprecious stones, from tortoiseshell and ivory to coral and exotic hardwoods. Pink coral was placed against black onyx or green chalcedony, while turquoise was combined with violet amethyst, and blue topaz with yellow citrine. Other materials included lapis lazuli, rock crystal and tiger's eye, all often offset with diamonds. These hard and semiprecious gemstone elements were sometimes frosted, sometimes carved into fluted spiralling patterns, and, in certain instances, both frosted and carved. Other examples – the more lavish ones – were made of chains either entirely set with diamonds or encrusted with fine-coloured precious gemstones, often fashioned *en cabochon*. Indian and Mughal Islamic motifs were a notable source for the design of their large pendants.

All these *sautoirs*, irrespective of the type and quality of the gems, and including those lavishly set with diamonds, were made of yellow gold (*see p 187*). This was a real

break with tradition; since the 18th century, whenever diamonds had been the focus of an ornament, they were invariably set in white metal to increase their whiteness. The ubiquitous use of gold in the 1970s was due to a number of reasons: firstly, the influence of traditional Indian jewels, where diamonds were always mounted in yellow gold; secondly, a desire to render diamonds more casual and wearable at any time of the day. The solar, warm colour of yellow gold, in contrast to the cool, nocturnal sheen of platinum, has been always associated with day-time jewelry and a more informal style. Remarkably, although 1970s *sautoirs* and their 1920s precursors share a number of similar features – such as length, successions of geometrical motifs, an Oriental decorative repertoire and unusual colour combinations, often obtained by unconventional juxtapositions of precious and semiprecious materials – they were in fact very different. The *sautoirs* of the 1970s are exceptional in their three-dimensional rendering of decorative elements, in distinct contrast to the flat treatment of those of the 1920s, and for their use of gold rather than platinum. The style of these *sautoirs* was universal and jewelers in Paris and London, such as Van Cleef & Arpels and Kutchinsky, in Rome and New York, such as Bulgari and David Webb, all produced similar designs.

The Eighties: the New Emancipation

The decade of the 1980s, which was characterized by widespread economic prosperity in the West, was also one which saw profound changes in the social and professional role of women. The process of emancipation, begun in the early years of the century, had now reached the point where women were becoming well-established and respected in all aspects of the work-place. Both in life and in fiction the decade was notable for strong, capable women, such as the formidable Margaret Thatcher and the shrewd, glamorous Alexis Carrington of *Dynasty*, played by actress Joan Collins. This new type of woman naturally adopted styles of dress that reflected her changed role. The ethnic, romantic look favoured in the 1970s was now replaced by clothes which could accommodate the busy lifestyle of the executive business woman yet still look attractive. Highly structured, tailored suits were favoured for all occasions, since they could be worn from morning till night, from boardroom to the opera. The 1980s woman, in her quest to succeed in a male-dominated environment, communicated her determination and assertiveness through 'power dressing' (*see pp. 190-191*). Broad shoulders, the archetypal attribute of the strong man, were adopted by women, becoming such a feature of contemporary fashion and so grotesquely exaggerated that the resulting female silhouette sometimes resembled that of an American football player.

Jewelry followed suit: it became bold both in design and size and served as yet another manifestation of the newly gained status and power of women. In the past, women had been the recipients of jewelry, both as tokens of love and as symbols of the status of their spouses. Now, with their newly acquired economic independence, women were in a position not only to choose but also to purchase their own jewels.

The executive woman of the 1980s, the archetypal female figure of the decade, required practical neck ornaments; these had to be decorative, but at the same time easy to wear in order not to interfere with an active lifestyle. Just as the tailored suit could be worn from morning until night, so the new necklace became a jewel that 'a woman can wear … to a ball or to a picnic', as Nicola Bulgari stated when commenting on their production in the 1980s in the American edition of *Vogue* in October 1995. 'Wearability' was now a key element in the design and construction of all jewels. The long swinging *sautoir* of the 1970s was inevitably eclipsed by short, sleek necklaces which perfectly complemented the tailored, structured line of contemporary dress.

Collars worn at the base of neck were unquestionably the favourite form of neck ornament of the decade. The typical design consisted of a wide convex band of metal and gemstones in which the decorative elements were an integral part of the structure. Pendants were excluded and the outline was always neat and sleek. When penannular in shape, these collars were fitted with springs to allow them to encircle the neck snugly and were often worn in multiples, one above the other. Some of the most representative examples of this style were created by the designer Marina B (*see pp. 190-191*). Another variation on the theme of the short collar was introduced by Bulgari; this consisted of gems mounted on coloured silk cords rather than on gold and gem-encrusted collars. Their decoration was largely based on the play of rounded geometrical motifs; even when naturalistic elements were included, they were stylized and contained within a geometrical framework.

Apart from those necklaces made up largely of yellow gold and diamonds, the range of colours and their various combinations were very wide indeed. Delicate yellow, pale-pink and light-blue sapphires or light-green emeralds were combined with a variety of other coloured stones, such as purple amethysts, red tourmalines and blue topazes. This more studied palette did, however, differ from the more garish and obvious one of the 1970s. The rounded forms of such designs were often complemented by stones being fashioned *en cabochon*; spiky claws were replaced by sleek collet settings. Buff-top calibrated coloured gemstones, rarely seen in jewelry since the 1920s, came back to serve the same purpose.

In addition to colourful gemstones, antique coins also featured on necklaces of the time. These were treated just like precious gems and often offset by a surround of diamonds or by a border of a differently coloured metal. Contrast between variously coloured metals is another notable feature of these necklaces, in which yellow, white and pink gold are often combined with steel and blackened gold.

Yet another fashionable type of necklace of the period was a single strand of exceptionally large cultured pearls referred to as 'South Sea' pearls, reflecting their origin in the warm waters off Burma, Australia, Indonesia and the Philippines (*see pp. 188-189*). This type of necklace had all the eighties' prerequisites of 'wearability', boldness of form and sleek outline. The exceptionally large pearls are produced by large, wild and rare species of saltwater oyster, *pinctada maxima*, of uncertain supply. This rarity explains

Opposite and below Haute couture designs for *tailleurs*. Valentino, Rome, autumn-winter collection, 1983–84.

A diamond necklace designed as a row of oval-shaped diamonds, weighing a total of 98.22 carats, the front supporting a D colour and Internally Flawless heart-shaped diamond of 56.42 carats, Graff, London, 1995.

why South Sea pearls, which usually measure from 10mm in diameter and are produced in a variety of colours from white to black, from silvery green to gold, are expensive; fine examples of such necklaces are exceptionally rare. Usually cultivated for longer periods than other pearls, South Sea pearls are rarely perfectly round and unblemished.

The 1980s also witnessed a return to the exclusive production of lavish, expensive necklaces set with exceptionally rare stones whose flawless qualities would be supported by gemmological certification (*see p. 192*). Not surprisingly, the design of such pieces was fairly traditional. They included *rivières* supporting large pendants, successions of floral clusters, and V-shaped bibs, where the size and shape of the gemstones governed the design. The object of such necklaces was to show off the stones, and the mounts had a purely functional role. This explains why the stones were held by minute claws which, in the case of high-colour diamonds, were always in white metal. The conventional design of these necklaces is an inevitable consequence of their incredibly high intrinsic value, never conducive to experimentation, and an indication of the taste of the limited clientèle in the position to afford them. Harry Winston in New York and Graff in London were the principal promoters of the trend.

The Nineties and Beyond

In the 1990s, in line with a more restrained economic climate, the mood in fashion has become more understated. The power dressing of the 1980s has been replaced by a more discreet style which seems to be reflected in recent jewelry. Necklaces remain short, but the collar is developing into softer, more feminine shapes. The vogue for yellow gold has begun to subside in favour of white gold and platinum. Coloured gemstones are now used more sparingly in less brash combinations. The deconstructed line in dress, typical of mid 1990s fashion, might also lead once again to the return of the *sautoir*. What is certain is that the necklace, a form of adornment over 30,000 years old, shows no sign of falling in popularity. It remains as alive, as exciting, as decorative and as beautiful as ever.

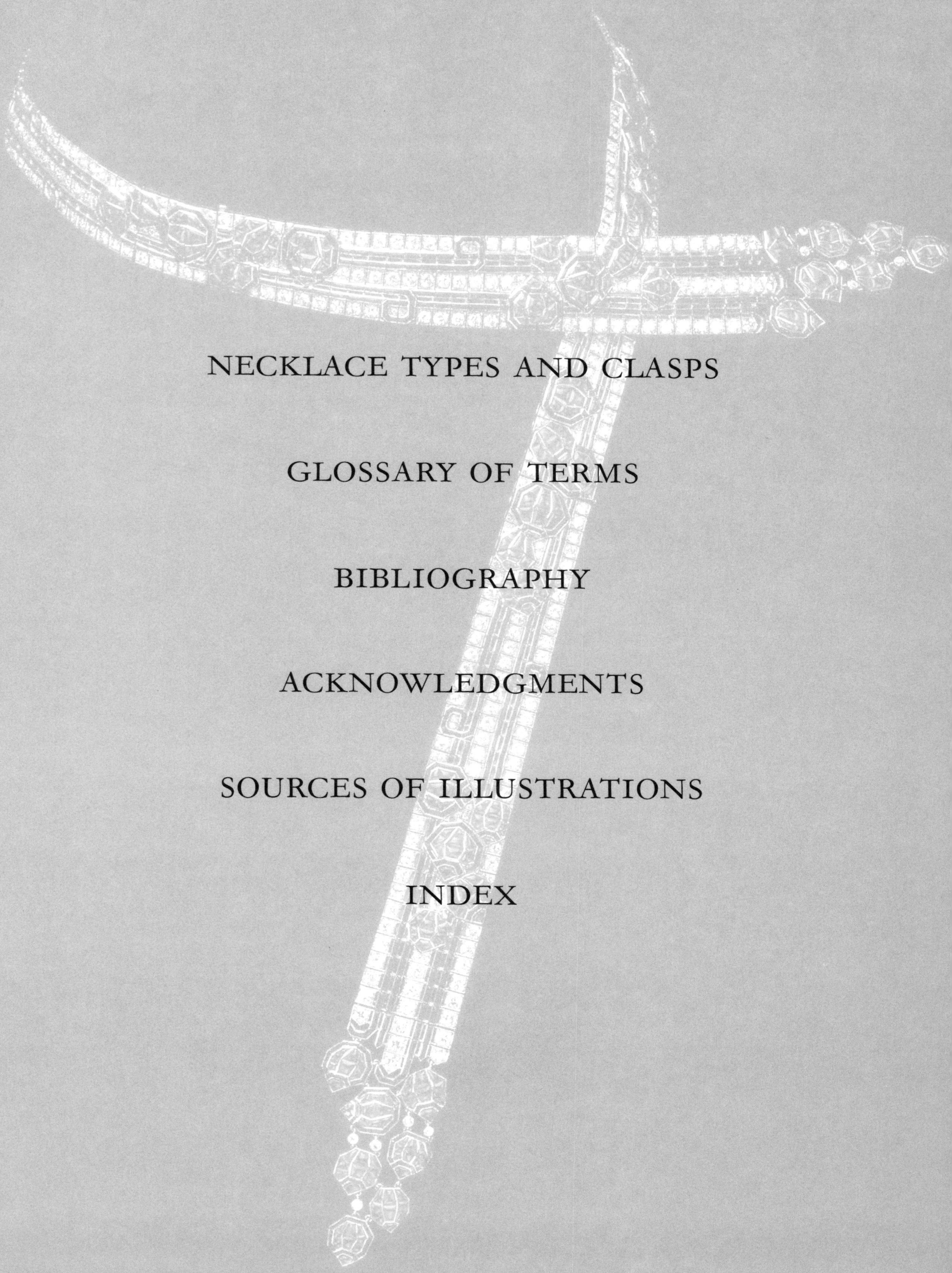

NECKLACE TYPES AND CLASPS

GLOSSARY OF TERMS

BIBLIOGRAPHY

ACKNOWLEDGMENTS

SOURCES OF ILLUSTRATIONS

INDEX

Necklace Types and Clasps

CHOKERS AND SHORT NECKLACES

Choker, dog dollar or *collier de chien*, are the terms commonly used to define the tight-fitting necklaces worn close around the neck which were fashionable during the last decades of the 19th century and the first of the 20th. The simplest form consisted of a jeweled central plaque (*plaque de cou*) applied either on to fabric or flanked by numerous rows of pearls (*see pp. 162–163*). The more lavish type was formed of a continuous articulated band entirely set with gemstones (*see pp. 134–135*). Both types were often very wide and were constructed to fit the shape and size of the neck of the wearer. The fashion for chokers was prompted by the contemporary vogue for evening dresses with a deep *décolletage*. These chokers were often worn with several other neck ornaments draped at the base of the neck and on the *décolletage* (*see p. 144*).

Tight-fitting necklaces worn high on the neck had been popular earlier, notably during the 18th century, when they consisted of articulated open-work bands of varying width set with a variety of gemstones. These jeweled bands either encircled the entire neck or just decorated the front of the neck. They were applied on to bands of fabric and were secured by means of tying either the fabric or the ribbon (threaded through metal loop terminals) to ensure a perfect fit around the neck. A number of examples supported detachable pendants and festoon motifs (*esclavage*) (*see pp. 70–71*).

In the 1980s short collars worn at the base of the neck were unquestionably the favourite form of neck ornament. The typical design consisted of a wide convex band of metal and gemstones in which the decorative elements were an integral part of the structure. When penannular in shape, these collars were fitted with springs to allow them to encircle the neck snugly. These last examples recall in shape the torcs of the early Celts (*see pp. 42–44*).

Platinum and diamond plaque on fifteen rows of seed pearls by
Lacloche, from the sale catalogue of the collection of jewels and
objets d'art belonging to Sultan Abd-ul-Hamid II, Paris, 1911.

Choker by René Lalique, *c.* 1900, in gold, carved opal, polychrome enamel and with a diamond plaque on fifteen rows of seed pearls.

Platinum and diamond plaque on ten rows of seed pearls with diamond-set space bars, by Cartier, Paris, *c.* 1910.

Design for a tight-fitting necklace formed of a triple row of stainless steel 'gas-pipe' linking studded with gold motifs, by Bulgari, Rome, 1984.

Design for a tight-fitting necklace formed of a triple row of gold 'gas-pipe' linking, the centre with a gem-set motif, by Bulgari, Rome, 1985.

Penannular flexible choker, by Marina B, 1987, formed of seven rows of cultured pearls, the central gem-set motif mounted with the famous Jonker no.8 diamond of 15.70 carats cut from the rough of 726 carats discovered at Elandsfontein, South Africa, in 1934.

FRINGE NECKLACES

Fringe necklace is the term used to define a neck ornament formed of pendent elements suspended either from a string or a chain of variously shaped links; these drops may be graduated in size from the centre to fit the contour of the base of the neck. The concept of stringing pendants to create body ornament goes back to the very origins of the necklace itself which dates from at least 30,000 B.C. The earliest and most impressive example of this type of necklace, however, dates from the mid 3rd millennium B.C. in Egypt, where it was known as the *wesekh* or broad collar. This was made up of several rows of cylindrical beads of stone or glazed composition graduated in size and vertically strung in an open-circle design between terminals of semi-circular shape (*see pp. 10–11*).

Minoan and Mycenaean necklaces of the 2nd millennium B.C. also conform to an overall fringe design. These were constructed as rows of stamped-out gold elements in the shape of volutes, leaves, rosettes, flowerheads, shells and figure-of-eight motifs (*see p. 16*).

Ancient Greek necklaces from the 7th century B.C. to the Hellenistic period (3rd-1st centuries B.C.) followed the fringe-type structure. These developed progressively from strings, from which were suspended gold embossed plaques, to the flexible gold mesh bands supporting multiple tears of variously shaped drops characteristic of the Hellenistic period (*see pp. 12–13*).

The Etruscans also favoured the fringe necklace. From the 7th century onwards Etruscan neck ornaments, whether designed as chains of gold mesh or formed of variously shaped beads, often supported pendants of extremely varied design (*see pp. 14–15*).

The fringe, so popular in antiquity, then almost completely disappeared for two millennia and only made its reappearance in the second half of the 19th century, possibly prompted by the contemporary taste for 'archaeological revival' jewelry. As in the past, the overall design consisted of a succession of pendent elements, at times graduated in size, but their tremendous variety in design is a distinguishing characteristic of the time: drops, leaves, amphorae, rosettes, seeds and fruiting grapes. Although gold was the favourite material for the rendering of these necklaces, semi-precious gemstones, enamels, cameos, intaglios, micromosaics and shells were also used (*see pp. 122–125*).

Fringe necklaces set mainly with diamonds became the vogue in the last quarter of the 19th century largely as a consequence of a greater abundance of the stones on the market. These were mounted in silver backed by gold and were often combined with pearls (*see pp. 130-131*).

In the 20th century the fringe necklace reappeared in the 1950s and has proved to be a popular type ever since. In particular it has been a successful form of necklace to display to great advantage large precious gem specimens (*see p. 192*).

An Egyptian polychrome faience bead
broad collar, from Tutankhamun's tomb,
c. 1333–1323 B.C.

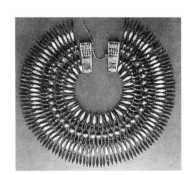

A Hellenistic gold fringe necklace, 3rd -2nd
centuries B.C., reproduced by Eugène
Fontenay in *Les Bijoux anciens et modernes*,
Paris, 1887.

Gold 'archaeological revival' fringe
necklaces, 1870s, suspending respectively
gold and seed pearl lanceolated drops,
polychrome micromosaic drops, and ivy-
leaf drops.

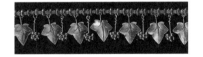

Gold and micromosaic 'archaeological
revival' fringe necklace, Italian, *c.* 1870,
supporting drops. The central drop depicts
Julius Caesar.

Gold 'archaeological revival' fringe necklace, by Ernesto Pierret, Rome, *c.* 1865, formed of a succession of triangular drops and baton-shaped motifs decorated with granulation and corded wire.

Diamond fringe necklace mounted in silver and gold, c. 1885, designed as a graduated fringe of drops and *fleur-de-lys* motifs set with cushion-shaped stones.

Diamond fringe necklace by Van Cleef & Arpels, New York, *c.* 1960, set with baguette, brilliant-cut and *marquise*-shaped stones, supporting fifteen larger step-cut diamonds.

RIVIÈRES AND CLUSTER NECKLACES

Rivière (stream) is the term commonly used to describe a necklace designed as a succession of gemstones individually set in simple collet or claw mounts without other ornamentation and often supporting a drop at the front. In general, the stones in a *rivière* are all of the same variety and are either graduated or all of the same size. As the most striking examples tend to be those mounted with diamonds, the term *rivière* is often used as a synonym for diamond-set neck ornament.

It is likely that the simple structure of the *rivière* was used for necklaces prior to the 18th century, but it was only in the second half of that century that the *rivière* came to the forefront of jewelry design. These were formed of a simple line of gemstones often graduated in size and mounted in plain closed collets. Early examples were generally strung on silk, while later examples have the collets connected to each other by small circular metal links.

By the turn of the century most *rivières* were set with gemstones mounted in open collets which remained the typical way of mounting until the end of the 19th century. In addition to diamonds, amethysts, citrines and agates were frequently mounted in the *rivières* of the period, which have survived in large numbers in their original form. This is due to their relatively low value in comparison with that of diamonds, which were often unmounted and reset. A distinguishing feature of late nineteenth-century *rivières* is the replacement of the earlier collets by claw settings.

This latter type of *rivière* was also extremely popular around 1900 and often worn together with the choker (*see p. 144*). Although by this time the *rivière* was an established form of necklace, its popularity subsided until the 1950s when alternatives to the circular brilliant-cut were introduced. *Rivières* came to be mounted with baguettes, step-cuts, oval and *marquise*-shaped diamonds, and in the 1980s with heart-shaped diamonds.

Necklaces designed as successions of clusters of gems rather than individual stones became fashionable from the late 18th century. This type of necklace which may be regarded as a more elaborate version of the *rivière* developed in a similar way (*see p. 80*). Cluster necklaces were fashionable throughout the 19th century and then, like *rivières*, were once again fashionable from the 1950s onwards.

Two diamond *rivières*; one (*above*) is set with cushion-shaped stones graduated in size from the centre, early 19th century; the other is set with rose-cut diamonds graduated from the centre, late 18th century.

Reverse of the two *rivières* pictured above; note the closed setting for the example dating to the 18th century, while the open setting is characteristic of later examples.

A gold and agate *rivière*, English, *c.*1800.

A diamond *rivière* collet-set with thirty-seven cushion-shaped diamonds graduated in size from the centre, English, 1820s. According to family tradition, this necklace was a gift from King George IV to his then mistress, Lady Conyngham.

An 1880s diamond necklace designed as a line of twenty-two circular clusters graduated in size from the centre, alternating with dart-shaped motifs, entirely set with cushion-shaped stones. As was the case with many examples of the time, the necklace doubles as a tiara with the appropriate fitting.

A diamond *rivière* entirely set with step-cut diamonds graduated in size from the centre, 1960s.

A diamond *rivière* by Cusi of Via Montenapoleone, Milan, *c.* 1972, set with a graduated line of oval stones, each claw-set in a concave white gold mount.

A diamond *rivière*, by Graff, London, 1990s, designed as a graduated row of heart-shaped diamonds, supporting two similar shaped D colour and Internally Flawless stones.

A Burmese ruby and diamond necklace by Harry Winston, New York, 1991. Designed as a line of thirteen ruby and diamond clusters supporting a detachable drop set with a ruby of 16.69 carats within a border of diamonds.

SAUTOIRS

Sautoir is a French term used since the beginning of the 19th century to describe a long neck ornament suspending a variously designed tassel or pendant. This form of ornament complements a vertical silhouette which explains why *sautoirs* have been in vogue at times when fashion has tended towards simple column-like garments. Long necklaces which hung down the chest and supported a pendant were worn by the Ancient Egyptians (*see p. 10*). These were made up of hardstone or gold strings of beads, single or multiple, which supported pendants decorated with polychrome gemstone inlays.

Although gold, enamel and gem-set longchains with suspended pendants were known in the second half of the 16th century (*see p. 46*) and again in the early years of the 19th century, the *sautoir* proper did not appear until around 1910 (*see pp. 140–141*). The *sautoirs* introduced at this time were formed mainly of bands or ropes of woven seed pearls supporting detachable pendants or tassels. The favourite gemstones were pearls and diamonds, mostly in *millegrain* settings. In time these evolved into the fashionable *sautoirs* of the 1920s, based on linear and geometrical designs, stylized naturalist decorative elements and gemstones of contrasting colours (*see pp. 166–167*). The polychromy and the eclectic decorative repertoire which ran from Chinese to Egyptian art was replaced in the late 1920s by *sautoirs* characterized exclusively by geometrical elements mainly set with diamonds. Often these examples could be divided into several bracelets and the pendants worn as brooches (*see pp. 164–165*).

The *sautoir* came back into vogue in the mid 1970s (*see pp. 186–187*). This time they were formed of either beads or of elongated links and supported large, often detachable pendants, conceived either as tassels or large versions of one of the elements of the *sautoir*. These frequently feature either colours and motifs of Indian inspiration or were made of unusual materials such as hardwoods, tortoiseshell, ivory with diamonds; they were always mounted in yellow gold.

Egyptian painted limestone relief at Bersha from the tomb of Djehuty-Hotpe in the reign of Senusret III, 1878–1841 B.C., depicting a woman wearing long neck ornaments suspending trapezoidal pendants.

Two ink designs for *sautoirs* by Holming for Fabergé; dated respectively 1909 and 1911, one with diamonds and calibrated rubies, the other with pearls and diamonds.

Design for a diamond and emerald *sautoir* by Van Cleef & Arpels, *c.* 1927 (*left*).

A 1970s pink coral, gold and diamond *sautoir*, by Van Cleef & Arpels, New York (*right*).

A 1970s cultured pearl, gold and diamond *sautoir*, by Van Cleef & Arpels, New York.

TRANSFORMABLE NECKLACES

The idea of designing a necklace in a manner that made it transformable into other types of ornament dates from the 18th century, although necklaces that could be adjusted in length and divided to be worn as bracelets did occur at earlier periods. During the 18th century the typical band necklaces of the time were embellished with festoon motifs and variously shaped pendants which could be removed. This allowed the wearer to wear the ornament in a reduced form (*see pp. 74–75*). The 1820s and 1830s were another period of popularity for this type of neck ornament. Necklaces at this time either of gold *cannetille* or of *repoussé*-work frequently featured detachable pendants which could be worn either as brooches and earrings. Also lavishly set necklaces of this time could be divided in segments wearable as bracelets.

The high point of this trend occurred in the last quarter of the 19th century when necklaces were designed to be divided into a multitude of ornaments which could be worn as brooches, rings or hair ornaments when secured to additional fittings. In addition, most necklaces of this period could be worn upside-down as tiaras when secured to the appropriate frames (*see pp. 120–121*). Similarly, the central plaque of chokers could be detached and worn separately as a brooch.

Versatility was also a feature of 1920s *sautoirs*, most of which could be shortened, divided and worn either as bracelets or head ornaments and epaulets. The pendants could be detached and worn as brooches or clips (*see p. 144*). This flexibility of use remained a feature throughout the 1930s and 1940s, when necklaces were often decorated with motifs which could be detached and worn either as clips or brooches, secured to bangles or even attached to a tiara fitting. The *passe-partout* necklace by Van Cleef & Arpels of 1939, which could be worn either as a necklace, bracelet or belt, stands as one of the most versatile necklace creations of all times (*see p. 178*).

In the 1950s Van Cleef & Arpels continued to favour versatility in necklaces by promoting their *fermeture éclaire* (zip) necklace. This could be literally zipped up and worn as a bracelet (*see p. 176*). From the 1960s onwards extreme versatility ceases to be a feature in neck ornaments.

A diamond necklace of interlaced circular motifs, English, 1820s (*above left*).

Reverse of the above necklace (*above right*), showing open setting and clasps which allow the necklace to be divided and worn as bracelets.

The three diamond bracelets which, joined together, form the necklace shown *above*.

Reverse of a diamond necklace, *c*. 1880 (*right, also illustrated on p. 120*), showing how the ornament may be divided to form a variety of smaller jewels when secured to the provided attachments. These include: a tiara fitting, three hair pins, seven brooch fittings, a ring and ear studs.

A pearl and diamond convertible necklace (*centre*), *c*. 1900; the central bow motif may be detached and worn as a brooch on the appropriate fitting; the pear-shaped pearl and diamond drops can be detached and may be worn on the *lavallière*.

This necklace divides into three bracelets, while the remaining segments may be worn as an epaulet secured by the brooch.

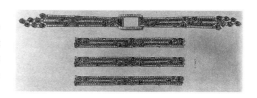

A ruby, onyx, emerald and diamond convertible necklace, by Boucheron, Paris, 1925, designed as a scarf of 86 cm in length.

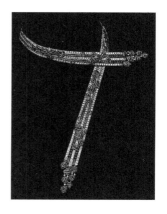

A gold and diamond convertible necklace, by Van Cleef & Arpels, Paris, 1937; the scale-like linking collar decorated at the front has two detachable diamond-set scroll motif clips.

An aquamarine, sapphire and diamond convertible necklace, by Cartier, Paris, 1939, set at the front with five detachable clips.

FASTENINGS AND CLASPS

The fastenings and clasps which secure the necklace around the wearer's neck have developed in time and often provide useful clues in the dating of pieces. Three main types of necklace fastenings can be distinguished. The earliest form consisted of the simple tying in a ribbon bow knot of the terminals of the string on which the decorative elements were strung. This system was the common practice from the very earliest times until the 4th century B.C. in the Mediterranean world (*see p. 9*). During the Hellenistic period, from the 3rd century B.C. onwards, threading a cord through the rings fitted at each terminal of the necklace became the main form of fastening (*see pp. 12–13*). This type of fastening remained in vogue for centuries and was the most popular type from the 1400s until the 1780s. A characteristic feature of late seventeenth-century and eighteenth-century necklaces was the use of rectangular or D-shaped metal terminals (*see pp. 74–75, 76–77*).

Another system for fastening necklaces was also developed in Hellenistic times when, around 300 B.C., some necklaces were fitted with a ring at one end and a hook, often S-shaped, to create another decorative feature (*see p. 37*). This type of fastening became the most popular way of securing necklaces in

Roman and Byzantine times; it was revived in the second half of the 19th century in the wake of the 'archaeological revival' movement in jewelry (*see pp. 116–117*).

The clasp which consists of a sprung metal tongue which fits into a variously shaped slot , was introduced at the end of the 18th century and continues to be the most widely used system for securing necklaces. Although this mechanism has evolved very little in itself, jewelers have increasingly tried to conceal it, disguising it in a variety of fashions and incorporating it into the overall design of the necklace. In the 1930s the clasp placed at the back of the neck became a focal point of decoration to complement contemporary evening wear (*see pp. 158, 170–171*).

Above left Heart-shaped miniature of Maria Carolina, Queen of Naples, *née* Archduchess of Austria, *c.* 1800, shown wearing two pearl necklaces.
Above right The reverse of the miniature shows the ribbon bow fastenings.

Early metal spring fastening mechanism on
a necklace set with chrysoberyls,
Portuguese, *c.* 1780.

S-shaped hook-and-eye clasp of Hellenistic tradition, on a gold fringe necklace in the 'archaeological revival' style, by Carlo Giuliano, *c*. 1870.

A sprung metal clasp with rectangular slot on a gold and enamel necklace in the 'archaeological revival' style, by Carl Bacher, Austrian, late 19th century.

Design for a diamond necklace, by Carlo Illario e Fratelli, Valenza, *c*. 1935. The clasp is concealed at the back in a decorative motif which echoes that of the front.

Tubular metal sprung clasp with similarly shaped slot on a gold and diamond necklace, French, *c*. 1960.

COLLET A circular, square, hexagonal or otherwise shaped band of metal within which a gemstone is set.

COLLET SETTING A style of setting in which the stone is fitted into a circular, square, hexagonal or otherwise shaped 'box' made from a thin metal band or 'collet'.

DEVANT DE CORSAGE A stomacher, the large ornament worn on the bodice at certain periods during the 18th century, extending from the *décolletage* to the waistline.

FESTONNÉ DESIGN A style of design incorporating festoons.

FIBULA A type of ancient garment-fastener brooch, consisting usually of a straight pin coiled to form a spring and extended backwards to form a bow and a catch-plate in order to secure the pin.

GALLERY A strip of metal that is pierced in a continuous pattern and terminates at the top with a series of claws which secure the stone. Such strips became popular for gemstone setting in the last quarter of the 19th century.

GIRANDOLE A type of brooch, earring or pendant consisting, in its simplest form, of a cluster or a single circular stone surmount supporting three pear-shaped drops. There are several variations of the base design where the surmount assumes more elaborate shapes in the form of ribbon bows, sprays of leaves and flowers, sometimes embellished with hearts or doves, the trophies of love.

GRANULATION A gold-working technique in which minute spherical grains of gold wire are applied and invisibly soldered to a metal surface to form decorative patterns. The process of granulation was known to the goldsmiths of the eastern Mediterranean from as early as the 3rd millennium B.C., and was largely used by the Greeks and refined by the Etruscans. The technique was revived by nineteenth-century jewelers working in the archaeological style.

INTAGLIO A technique of gem carving where the stone is engraved below the level of its prepared flat and polished surface. The term is perhaps better understood if explained as the opposite of a cameo.

KNIFE WIRE A type of jewelry wire made with a sharp edge that is always turned upwards to reflect a thin line of bright light to provide an almost invisible setting which conveys a feeling of great lightness.

LAMINATE A sheet of metal made of two thin leaves of different metals, usually silver and gold, rolled together. Gold and silver laminate, with gold at the back and silver at the front, was used throughout the 19th century. This practice declined at the beginning of the 20th century, when platinum was introduced.

MARQUISE-SHAPED A modification of the brilliant-cut; the stone is elliptical and pointed at both ends with a hexagonal table surrounded on the crown by thirty-two trapezium-shaped and triangular facets. The pavilion has twenty-four facets and a culet. It is sometimes called *navette*.

MICROMOSAIC (*Roman mosaic*) A mosaic made of very small pieces - *tesserae* - of variously coloured glass inlaid in glass or hardstone plaques.

MILLEGRAIN SETTING A style of setting of a gem in which the stone is secured in the collet by a series of minute adjacent beads (grains) of metal which are raised by passing a knurling tool (*millegrain* tool) around the top edge of the collet.

ORIENT The iridescent lustre of the surface of a pearl and also of the nacreous lining (mother-of-pearl) of the shell of a mollusc.

PAMPILLE, EN A style of decorating jewelry in the form of articulated cascades of gemstones graduated in size from the top and terminating with tapered pointed drops.

PARURE A suite of matching jewelry, usually comprising a necklace, a pair of earrings and a bracelet; one or more brooches and a hair ornament are sometimes included.

PÂTE DE VERRE Literally, glass paste; material

produced by grinding glass to powder and then melting it in appropriate moulds by means of firing.

PAVÉ SETTING A style of setting gemstones in which many stones, usually of small dimension, are set very close to each other so as to cover the entire surface of the jewel, almost concealing the metal.

PENDELOQUE Usually a pear-shaped gemstone or a jewel; *pendeloque* earrings are designed as a *marquise*-shaped, oval or circular surmount supporting a ribbon bow motif and an elongated drop; they were particularly fashionable in the second half of the 18th century.

PIQUÉ-WORK A style of decoration of small objects of tortoiseshell made with inlaid minute points or strips of gold or silver.

PLASMA A variety of cryptocrystalline quartz (chalcedony) which is opaque and of various shades of green with white or yellowish spots.

PLIQUE-À-JOUR An enamelling technique which consists of outlining the design with metal and filling it with variously coloured transparent or translucent enamel but with no backing behind the enamel, so that the effect is similar to that of a stained-glass window.

REPOUSSÉ A technique of producing a relief decoration by means of raising the pattern from the reverse of the metal sheet with a punch and hammer. The work is done manually but often the term is used to describe the similar mechanical process of embossing by means of stone or metal dies.

RÉSILLE Network: in jewelry, a network of beads, pearls or gemstones.

TESSERA (pl. *tesserae*) The small cubes or blocks which make up mosaics.

TABLE-CUT The style of cutting a diamond by removing the natural points of an octahedral crystal, leaving a flat, square or rectangular table at the top and a similar but smaller parallel flat surface (the culet) at the bottom.

Bibliography

A Sparkling Age, 17th Century Diamond Jewellery (exhibition catalogue), Antwerp, 1993

ALDRED, C., *Jewels of the Pharaoh*, London, 1971

ANDREWS, C., *Ancient Egyptian Jewellery*, London, 1990

BECKER, V., *Antique and Twentieth-Century Jewellery*, London, 1980 (1st ed.), 1987 (2nd ed.)

BECKER, V., *Art Nouveau Jewelry*, London, 1985

BECKER, V., *The Jewellery of René Lalique* (exhibition catalogue), London, 1987

BENNETT, D., MASCETTI, D., *Understanding Jewellery*, Woodbridge, 1989

BLACK, A., *Storia dei Gioielli*, Novara, 1973

BRADFORD, E., *Four Centuries of European Jewellery*, London, 1953

BURY, S., *Jewellery Gallery Summary Catalogue*, Victoria and Albert Museum, London, 1983

BURY, S., *Jewellery 1789-1910, The International Era*, Woodbridge, 1991

CAILLES, F., *René Boivin Joaillier*, Paris, 1994

Cartier, splendeurs de la joaillerie (exhibition catalogue), Lausanne, 1996

CARTLIDGE, B., *Twentieth-Century Jewelry*, New York, 1985

CARUSO, I., *Collezione Castellani: Le Oreficerie*, Rome, 1988

COLOGNI, F., NUSSBAUM, E., *Platinum by Cartier, Triumphs of the Jewelers' Art*, New York, 1996

CRISTOFANI, M., MARTELLI, M., *L'oro degli Etruschi*, Novara, 1983

CULME, J., RAYNER, N., *The Jewels of the Duchess of Windsor*, London, 1987

EVANS, J., *A History of Jewellery 1100-1870*, London, 1953 (1st ed.), 1970 (2nd ed.)

FLOWER, M., *Victorian Jewellery*, London, 1951

FONTENAY, E., *Les Bijoux anciens et modernes*, Paris, 1887

FREGNAC, C., *Jewellery from the Renaissance to Art Nouveau*, London, 1965

GABARDI, M., *Les Bijoux de l'Art Déco aux Années 40*, Paris, 1980

GABARDI, M., *Gioielli Anni '50*, Milan, 1986

GERE, C., *Victorian Jewellery Design*, London, 1982

GERE, C., *European and American Jewellery*, London, 1985

GERE, C., RUDOE, J., TAIT, H., WILSON, T., *The Art of the Jeweller, A Catalogue of the Hull Grundy Gift to the*

British Museum, London, 1984

Gli Ori di Taranto in Età Ellenistica (exhibition catalogue), Milan, 1984

GOREWA, O., POLYNINA, I., RACHMANOV, N., RAIMANN, A., *Joyaux du Trésor de Russie*, Paris, 1991

GREGORIETTI, G., *Il Gioiello nei Secoli*, Milan, 1969

HACKENBROCH, Y., *Renaissance Jewellery*, Munich, 1979

HAUSER KOCHERT, I., *Köchert Jewellery Designs 1810-1940*, Florence, 1990

HIGGINS, R., *Greek and Roman Jewellery*, London, 1961

HIGGINS, R., *Minoan and Mycenaean Art*, revised edition, London, 1981

HINKS, P., *Nineteenth-Century Jewellery*, London, 1975

HINKS, P., *Twentieth-Century Jewellery 1900-1980*, London, 1983

HOFFMAN, H., DAVIDSON, P., *Greek Gold*, Brooklyn, 1965

KOCH, M., *et al.*, *The Belle Époque of French Jewellery 1850-1910*, London, 1990

KRASHES, L., *Harry Winston: The Ultimate Jeweler*, New York, 1984 (1st ed.), 1986 (2nd ed.), 1988 (3rd ed.)

KUNZ, G.F. & STEVENSON, C.H., *The Book of the Pearl*, New York, 1908, (reprinted 1993)

LAVER, J., *Costume and Fashion. A Concise History*, London, 1988

Les Fouquets, Bijoutiers & Joailliers à Paris 1860-1960 (exhibition catalogue), Musée des Arts Décoratifs, Paris, 1983

LIGHTBOWN, R. W., *Mediaeval European Jewellery*, London, 1992

MASCETTI, D., TRIOSSI, A., *Bulgari*, Milan, 1996

MASCETTI, D., TRIOSSI, A., *Earrings, From Antiquity to the Present*, London, 1990

MEDVEDEVA, G., PLATONOVA, N., POSTNIKOVA-LOSEVA, M., SMORODINOVA, G., TROEPOLSKAYA, N., *Russian Jewellery 16th-20th Centuries from the Collection of the Historical Museum, Moscow*, Moscow, 1987

MOREL, B., *The French Crown Jewels*, Antwerp, 1988

MULLER, P.E., *Jewels in Spain 1500-1800*, New York, 1972

MUNN, G., *Castellani and Giuliano, Revivalist Jewellers of the Nineteenth Century*, London, 1984

NADELHOFFER, H., *Cartier: Jewellers Extraordinary*, London and New York, 1984

NERET, G., *Boucheron, Four Generations of a World-Renowned Jeweller*, Paris, 1988

O DAY, D., *Victorian Jewellery*, London, 1974 (1st ed.), 1982 (2nd ed.)

OGDEN, J., *Jewellery of the Ancient World*, London, 1982

Ori e Argenti di Sicilia (exhibition catalogue), Milan, 1989

PHILLIPS, C., *Jewelry: from Antiquity to the Present*, London, 1996

PIERIDES, A., *Jewellery in the Cyprus Museum*, Cyprus, 1971

Princely Magnificence: Court Jewels of the Renaissance, (exhibition catalogue), London, 1980

PRODDOW, P., HEALE, D., *American Jewelry, Glamour and Tradition*, New York, 1987

RAULET, S., *Art Déco Jewelry*, Paris, 1984

RAULET, S., *Van Cleef & Arpels*, Paris, 1986

RAULET, S., *Bijoux des Années 1940-1950*, Paris, 1987

RYBAKOV, B.A., (ed.), *Treasures of the USSR Diamond Fund*, Moscow, 1980

SCARISBRICK, D., *Jewellery*, London, 1984

SCARISBRICK, D., *Tudor and Jacobean Jewellery*, London, 1985

SCARISBRICK, D., *Ancestral Jewels*, London, 1989

SCARISBRICK, D., *Jewellery in Britain, 1066-1837, A Documentary, Social, Literary and Artistic Survey*, Wilby, Norwich, 1994

SCARISBRICK, D., *Chaumet, Master Jeweller since 1780*, Paris, 1995

SNOWMAN, K., *Carl Fabergé*, London, 1980

SNOWMAN, K., *et al.*, *The Master Jewelers*, London, 1990

SNOWMAN, K., *Fabergé: Lost and Found, The Recently Discovered Jewelry Designs from the St. Petersburg Archives*, Milan, 1990, London, 1993

SOLODKOFF, A., *Masterpieces from the House of Fabergé*, New York, 1994

STEINGRAEBER, E., *Antique Jewellery, its History in Europe from 800 to 1900*, London, 1957

STREETER, E., *A Catalogue of Designs*, Harlow, 1992 (Facsimile ed. of 60th ed., *c.* 1885)

TAIT, H. (ed.), *Seven Thousand Years of Jewellery*, London, 1986

TILLANDER, H., *Diamond Cuts in Historic Jewellery, 1381-1910*, London, 1995

VEVER, H., *La Bijouterie française au XIXe siècle*, Paris, 1908

WILLIAMS, D., OGDEN, J., *Greek Gold, Jewellery of the Classical World* (exhibition catalogue), London, 1994

Acknowledgments

We would like to thank all those who have generously provided us with information, suggestions, and advice, as well as copious photographic material, and who have given us support and encouragement throughout our research:

Mr and Mrs Franklin Adler, Adler, Geneva; Gilbert Albert, Geneva; Maria Serena Joyeria Bagués, Barcelona; Serena Battaglia, Istituto Geografico de Agostini, Milan; Victor Franco de Baux, London; Tiziana Bellucci, Marina B, Geneva; Bernard Berger, Cartier S.A., Geneva; Goriviano Bernardini, Bulgari, Rome; Susi Billingsley, Valentino Couture, Rome; Dorothy Bosomworth, Cartier Ltd., London; Yves Brasseur, Sint-Martens-Latem; Mr De Breyne, Deinze; Clarissa Bruce, London; Marina Bulgari Spaccarelli, Marina B, Geneva; François Canavy, Van Cleef & Arpels, Paris; Anne Choate, Christie's, Geneva; Letizia Corinti, Bulgari, Rome; Lois Cox, London; Lydia Cresswell-Jones, Sotheby's, London; Sandra Cronan, London; Giampaolo Della Croce, Bulgari, Rome; Arthur and Ria Dietschweiler, St Gallen; Lionel Dorléans, Courbevoie; Tom Eden, Sotheby's, London; Danielle Enoch, Sotheby's, London; Jaqueline Fay, Sotheby's, New York; Tessa Ferguson, Antique Collector's Club Ltd., Woodbridge; Angela Folino, Christie's, New York; Oliver Forge, Sotheby's, London; Rosemary Forrester, Melbourne; Melissa Gabardi, Milan; Caroline Gardaz, Christie's, Geneva; Philippe Garner, Sotheby's, London; Elisabetta Genuizzi, Walpole Gallery, London; Christopher Gow, Sotheby's, New York; Laurence Graff, Graff, London; Andrew and Jojo Grima, Farnese S.A., Gstaad; Emmanuel Guillaume, E.S.G., Antwerp; Hennell of Bond Street, London; Lucy Hodson, Sotheby's, London; Nigel Israel, London; Betty Jais, Cartier S. A., Paris; Gwendoline Keywood, Graff, London; Laurence S. Krashes, Harry Winston, New York; Clarisse La Fonta, Mellerio *dits* Meller, Paris; Isabelle de La Mussaye, Sotheby's, Geneva; Marie Chantal Ladenius, Lugano; Lia Lenti, Valenza; Isabel Léonard, Van Cleef & Arpels, Paris; Gian Luca Illario, Carlo Illario & Fratelli, Valenza; Claire Marmion, Sotheby's, London; Kieran McCarthy, Wartski, London; Elizabeth Mitchell, Sotheby's, London; Geoffrey Munn, Wartski, London; Eric Nussbaum, Cartier Joaillerie S.A., Geneva; Michael Oldford, New York; Lillian Ostergard, Verdura, New York; Stefano Papi, Sotheby's, Milan; Stefano Peccatori, Elemond, Milan; Lucilla Phelps, London; S.J. Phillips, London; John Quinn, London; Alexandra Rhodes, Sotheby's, London; Chantal Röthlisberger Brasseur, Sint-Martens-Latem; Raymond Sancroft-Baker, Christie's, London; Alexei Sapsford, London; Philip Sapsford, London; Diana Scarisbrick, London; Rita Severis, Sotheby's, Nicosia; Inez Stodel, Amsterdam; Hugh Tait, London; Suzanne Tennenbaum, Malibu, California; Michèle Tonnelot, Boucheron, Paris; William Trebilcok, New York; Danièle Turrian, Sotheby's, Geneva; Violante Valdettaro, Valentino Couture, Rome; Jean-Pierre Varin, Cretec, Paris; Studio Vivi Papi, Varese; Valerie Vlasaty, Sotheby's, New York; Valerie Westcott, Sotheby's, New York; Jurg Wille, Zurich; Hayden Williams, Sotheby's, London; Lorraine Williams, New York; Jennifer Winn, Sotheby's, New York; Paola Zagari, Naples.

Sources of Illustrations

a: above, b: bottom, c: centre, l: left, r: right

Historisch Museum, Amsterdam 66-7a; Marina B, Geneva 191; Cecil Beaton Photograph, courtesy of Sotheby's, London 160, 165ar&br, 184ar, 193; Rheinisches Landesmuseum, Bonn 42ar; Archives Boucheron, Paris 132, 133, 135a, 144c&b, 161, 176cr, 180al, 181, 186l, (Photo Lionel Dorléans, Courbevoie) 201 & 213br; Courtesy Chantal Brasseur and M. De Breyne 63b; Moravské Muzeum, Brno 9al; Bulgari Archives, courtesy Bulgari, Rome 184ar&b, 203cl; Egyptian Museum, Cairo (Photo Albert Shoucair) 10al, (Werner Forman Archive) 11b, 17, 210a; Courtesy of the Fogg Art Museum, © President and Fellows, Harvard College, Harvard University Art Museums, Cambridge. Gift of the Estate of Harriet Anna Niel 97bl; *Catalogue of The Goldsmiths & Silversmiths Company Ltd*, London, 1901 95a, 131br; Chi Mei Cultural Foundation, Taiwan 112al; Christie's, Geneva 102cl; Christie's, London 79b, 121b; Christie's, New York 107, 111, 140-141ac, 154; Courtesy Sandra Cronan, (Photo Lucilla Phelps), London 78; Published by permission of the Director of Antiquities and the Cyprus Museum 9bl&br, 16b, 36a&b, 39bl&br, 40; © Michael Duigan 11ar; Courtesy Electa, Milan 62, 70b; Galleria degli Uffizi, Florence 44bl, 49; Château de Fontainebleau, (© Photo RMN) 99bl; E. Fontenay, *Les Bijoux anciens et modernes*, Paris, 1887 56, 101cr&br, 205c; Graff, London Archives. Courtesy Graff, London 149, 200, 209a; Andrew Grima Collection, (Photo J. Quinn), London 182; *Harper's*, vol.46 63a; Hennell of Bond Street, London (Photo J. Quinn) 112ar; Archives Carlo Illario e Fratelli, Valenza 172cl, 185l; Israel Department of Antiquities, Israel Museum, Jerusalem 9ar; Badisches Landesmuseum, Karlsruhe 98a; G.F.Kunz and C.H.Stevenson, *The Book of the Pearl*, New York, 1908 94, 144al, 151l; Courtesy Antiquarium Lavinium 26, 27; By permission of The British Library, London 51; Copyright British Museum, London 13c&ar, 33a, 37b, 38, 39a&c, 41b, 42al&br, 43b; By courtesy of the Board of Trustees of the Victoria & Albert Museum, London 65, 70a, 71l, 72, 76, 77, 88, 98b, 100, 153; Museo del Prado, Madrid 48ar; Mappin & Webb Ltd catalogue, London, 1901 146; Masreria, Barcelona, Jojaria Bagués 128; Mellerio, Paris 87l, 90, 125, 135b; Museo Poldi Pezzoli, Milan 45br; *Les Modes*, Paris, 1909 151r; Arnoldo Mondadori Editore, Milan 36c, 37ar&c; Bayerisches National Museum, Munich 47b; Copyright The Frick Collection, New York 73l; The Metropolitan Museum of Art, New York (Photo Peter Clayton) 10b, (Bequest of Benjamin Altman 1913) 45ar; Istituto Geografico de Agostini, Novara 14-15, 34-5; Ashmolean Museum,

Index